artefact

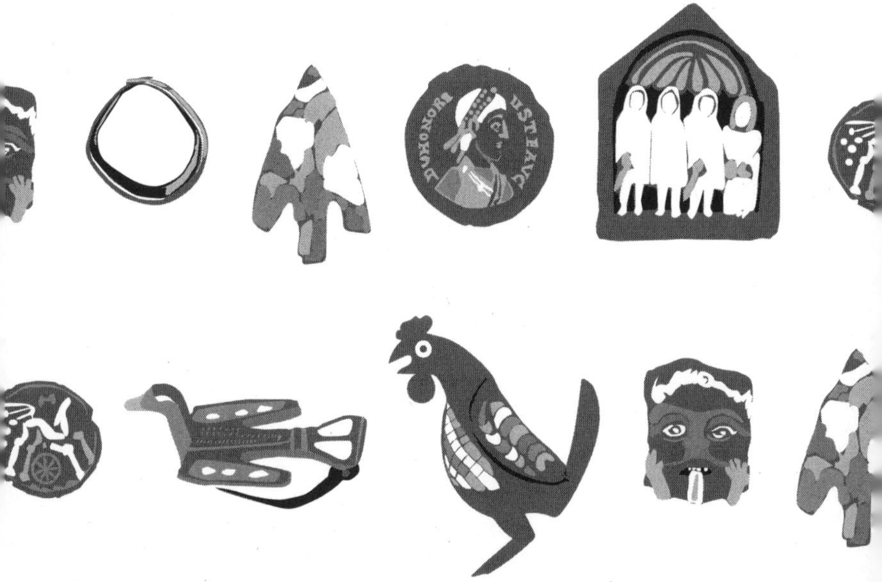

Featuring

CARLOS ALMONACID	ROSE LEICESTER
ROSAMUND BROWN	ROSE LENNARD
AMARIS CHASE	HARRIET MCDONALD
HILDA COCHRANE	REBECCA MCDOWALL
LUCY DALGLEISH	MARY MOORE
ANDREW DONALDSON	ROSALIND NEWTON
HENRY DAVIES	CHARLOTTE PAYNE
VICKI FLETCHER	GRAHAM POWELL
CHLOE HALL	ANGELA REDDAWAY
ALICE HART	MARGARET ROYALL
JONATHAN HART	STUART SAMUEL
CHLOE HEADDON	SHARON WEBSTER
HEIDI HOWARTH	JULIE WILTSHIRE
VENETIA JOHANNES	

with a foreword by
EMMA STUART
Director of the Corinium Museum, Cirencester

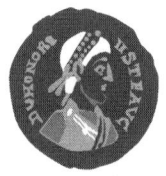

Ancient myths and Roman treasures,
lost loves and haunted relics: historical objects
reimagined in fiction, memoir and poetry

artefact

illustrated with photographs from the
CORINIUM MUSEUM COLLECTION

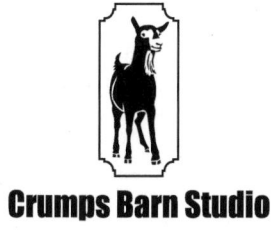

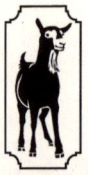

Crumps Barn Studio

visit: crumpsbarnstudio.co.uk

in collaboration with

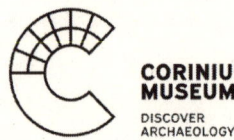

coriniummuseum.org

Crumps Barn Studio
Syde, Cheltenham GL53 9PN
www.crumpsbarnstudio.co.uk

Text copyright © the authors and Crumps Barn Studio 2024
Photographs and their descriptions copyright © Cotswold District
Council, courtesy of Corinium Museum, Cirencester

The rights of the named authors to be identified as the authors of this work has been asserted in accordance with the Copyright, Designs and Patents Act 1988.

All rights reserved. No part of this publication may be reproduced, stored in a retrieval system, or transmitted in any form or by any means, electronic, mechanical, photocopying, recording or otherwise, without the prior permission of the copyright owner.

Cover design and illustrations by Lorna Gray

Typeset in Adobe Garamond Pro

All our books are printed on responsibly sourced paper from managed woodlands and recycled material. Printed in the UK by CMP, Poole

ISBN 978-1-915067-65-4

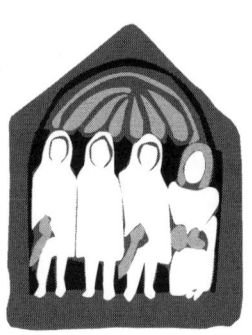

Foreword

When you hold an ancient object in your hand, something happens. There is an appreciation of it whether it is a beautiful, complete statue or a small fragment of pottery found lying on the surface of a field. There is a magical connection, not just to the object but to the maker, to the owner and to its final resting place under the ground or to its current home. Such objects connect you to the past, to the people who lived long ago and to a spirit of place.

In the museum we have a statue of a Genius Loci. A figure who represents the spirit of place. He holds a bowl called a patera in one hand and a cornucopia in the other. This altar was set up with the intention of blessing and protecting the land, the cornucopia metaphorically spilling its abundance, and to connect the local people to their surrounding landscape. Now removed from its original position, it sits in the museum, often overlooked by visitors but, for me at least, it still emits an aura communicating its original intention.

To see that these artefacts have the power to inspire writers, artists, craftspeople and designers is just wonderful. It reinforces my career path, as one of a team of people responsible for caring for, preserving, displaying and interpreting these very special items, spanning the Palaeolithic to post medieval periods. That intangible gift of imagination is evident through the poetry and prose people have created in this anthology. It's a very special moment when ancient objects and places provide the necessary spark to allow that creative journey to commence. It has been a true pleasure to read the stories and poetry inspired by objects from the Corinium Museum collections and from elsewhere.

Emma Stuart, Museum Director
Corinium Museum, Cirencester

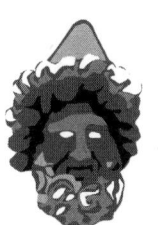

Modal Ambition

ROSAMUND BROWN

Had I the back for it,
I would be an archaeologist,
going into rhapsodies
over a trowel trawling through gravelly earth,
glancing oolitic limestone with a regular tuning note.
Descending the layers until I hit fifteenth century petrichor
(did they hope for rain? Had it been dry for weeks?).
The dankness of a wine cellar, but more intoxicating,
exclusive to the connoisseurs.

I would embrace the hi-vis,
the geophys,
the dirt-ingrained hands,
nails potted with loam like a miniature auricula theatre.
Worth the bizarre tan lines
for the complete clay pipes,
rare currency,
arrow heads,
lips of amphorae,
seal rings,
Matchbox Fords,
rough corner stones (an obligatory boundary wall);
I would get so close I would want to lick them,
or brush up loose soil and wash my face with it.

I would not deal well with infilling.
Had I the back for it,
I would want to roll around in the trench,
immerse myself in historical strata.

No need for it *always* to be a king in a carpark;
I would happily bruise my bones
        on Victorian household detritus,
sewer pipes,
imprinted half-bricks.
And if I did find a being
I would know to focus on the pelvis,
to gauge their sex,
and to gently caress their smooth and jagged fragments,
quietly reading them like beautiful braille.

Depicting the Divine

HEIDI HOWARTH

"Have you heard about the latest column capitals in Corinium, Pax?"

Mercury was smirking as Pax walked towards him. Pax's long ivory dress, adorned with embroidered olive branches, swept serenely over the stone floor, mirroring the flow of her loose tresses.

"Yes, I have. That is why I've come. Has everyone already been informed?" she asked.

"Not by me. Who has been depicted on what is not high on my agenda, though I must admit they have great taste in that town. I see another sculpture bearing my image has been proudly placed. Either way, I don't imagine Vulcan is aware. I see no fires raging … yet. But I know you'll be particularly concerned that he knows. Would you like me to deliver the news?"

A tapping sound echoed through Mercury's temple. He searched for the source and smiled at the sight of a deer trotting through the entrance, followed by a woman bearing a bow in her left hand and a quiver full of arrows on her back. She was wearing simple attire, paired with sturdy boots, in contrast to Pax's bare feet.

"I have no doubt Pax is best placed to deliver the message to Vulcan herself if we want a peaceful resolution," the huntress said, "I think such a conversation needs a delicate touch.

It is not that you are not tactful, but you have a reputation for not always using it, especially regarding your brother. I'm surprised you haven't told him he has made it onto a capital, just to see his hopes crushed when he sees he has not," she said slyly but with an air of playfulness in her voice.

"Ah, Diana, I didn't see you come in. I am surprised that the news of the town has reached you in the forest so quickly."

"The Gods have you as a messenger. I have my birds." she smiled. "I have a message for Vulcan myself. I had intended to employ your assistance in this matter, but perhaps you could deliver the good news, Pax, something to soften the blow of the capitals?"

"You can't use your birds for such a message? A seagull, perhaps, or are they only used for conversing with Neptune?" Mercury asked, straight-faced but with an air of supremacy.

"It is indeed my intention to deliver the news to Vulcan personally," Pax said. "I merely aim to spare you from Vulcan's ranting. I'm sure you have far more pressing matters to deal with than his resentment. If you would please send word to the others to keep the depiction business under wraps, though, it is important that they be told before words spread, which will be quick, but not nearly quick enough to rival your speed and agility, Mercury."

He smiled and nodded at them both, then swiftly departed. The two goddesses curtsied to one another in mutual respect before leaving for their respective duties – Diana's in the vastness of the wilderness, and Pax's in the stuffy seclusion of Vulcan's forge.

IT REGRETTABLY had not been centuries or even years

since Pax had last come to Vulcan's forge at Mount Etna, but mere days. The prosperity, urbanisation and cultural exchange that the time of Pax Romana brought – so named after her – meant an increase in the creation of things. Yet, with all that creation, there had been an absence of Vulcan's depiction, in particular on Corinthian capitals that sat atop the large columns supporting many of the structures in emerging settlements. As Vulcan believed he supported the people's abilities to craft such structures with his tools, and as there was no God of masonry, he felt he would be the fitting deity to adorn them, but he very rarely was. A point he was becoming increasingly and more frequently sour about.

He was often resentful of the other gods, owing to his mother's shallow rejection of him as a child and the adulterous betrayal by his wife Venus with his brother Mars. Unlike many of the other celebrated Gods, Vulcan was not blessed by beauty or grace, but his metalwork skills offered so much more to the people, and so he thought they ought to be punished for their lack of acknowledgement of his mastery of them. But every request he had made, from asking Neptune to cause earthquakes to his pleas to Ceres to neglect their crops, had all been refused. And with each snub made by the people and refusal from the gods to punish them, Pax would need to go and mend the burnt bridges and make things between the gods harmonious again.

Today, like most days she came to visit, he was in his forge alone, working away at some new tool that was no doubt destined for one of Rome's heroes.

"Greetings, Vulcan," she said as he acknowledged her presence with a quick glance before returning his focus to his work. He turned the glowing, would-be blade, placed it on its thickest side onto the anvil, and struck it with his hammer. He examined it with precision, taking in the geometry of it, but he needed no other tool than his eye to measure the alignment of the taper to the point or the main bevel angle. After a few moments and some adjustments with his grinding stone, he plunged the sword into the quenching bucket filled with oil. A cloud of steam shrouded him from Pax's view.

"Salve, Pax," he replied.

"How have you been? Working on something new?" she asked hesitantly, unable to read his mood behind the cover of the rising steam.

"Always working on something new," he said matter-of-factly. "I appreciate the small talk, but I'm rather busy." He nodded to his bucket, which was now simmering instead of steaming. Pax could now see him, but she was none the wiser as to his current temper. He gave nothing away. "Is there something I can help you with?"

"I have some news to share with you. A copper alloy has been crafted in your image in the town of Corinium. It is a fitting ode to your skill with fire and forge."

"Corinium, is it a significant settlement?"

"Very much so. It is a hub for trade and commerce. The people seem to honour the Gods appropriately. A sign of truly understanding and appreciating the Gods, wouldn't you agree?"

"Many Statues of Mercury, then, is what you mean to allude to."

"Of course, he is rather relevant there owing to his

association with travel and trade. This is why I bring you news of your inclusion. It is not often they honour other gods. I also have a message from Diana. She offers her thanks. Without your advice, she would not have been able to safeguard the sacred groves and wildlife in the surrounding areas from the forest fire near the Tiber River."

The corners of his mouth shifted slightly upwards, and Pax relaxed her shoulders, although her relief proved premature.

"And what of the capitals in Corinium?" he asked.

"I will not insult you with the pretence that I do not know why you ask. I respect you too much for that," she said. She didn't gush at him with her flattery but simply presented it as if it were fact, knowing he did not entertain such falseness. "I will gladly save you the trouble of leaving your forge – if you promise to keep your frustrations within it. I am happy to listen, but no more asking the gods for punishment. It will only cause bad blood between you, and I know they value you and your work too much to want that to happen. They need you, Vulcan." She said gently, expertly bolstering his ego without raising suspicion.

He nodded in agreement to her terms.

"Bacchus, Silenus, Lycurgus and Ambrosia are the latest additions."

His face, if it were not already red and sweat-covered from the heat of the forge, would have turned so. "The disrespect is beyond belief. That these ... these people of Corinium would value frivolity over diligent craftsmanship. They are nothing but a bunch of despicable pleasure-seekers!" He clenched his hammer, almost crushing the handle with his grip.

"Your skills of metalwork are being worshipped in

singular form, not as an afterthought. Why concern yourself with such trivial things as the capitals, Vulcan? They are mere minor additions to the spectacular, overshadowing columns they sit upon, and the buildings they sit under."

"A small alloy compared to a vast building. They are not the same," he grumbled.

"Buildings that without your skill, would cease to exist. Do you not see that every building the capitals help hold aloft is a direct testament to your skill? You are more than the sum of the capitals, Vulcan," she said softly. "You are the heartbeat of craftsmanship, the soul of creation."

"Perhaps." he sighed, wiping the sweat from his brow.

"Like the foundations of the buildings and Corinium itself is built upon – just because you are not seen, does not mean great thought is not given to your importance. Perhaps it is you who does not see your greatness reflected in that polished steel of yours."

Pax patiently waited as Vulcan swished his cooling weapon around in the oil. He looked up, meeting Pax's gaze with a mixture of gratitude and contemplation. And as the flames danced in the forge, casting their warm glow upon the jagged stone walls, the glow spread to Vulcan's eyes, and Pax knew that her message had been heard, and the matter of the capitals was closed, at least for now.

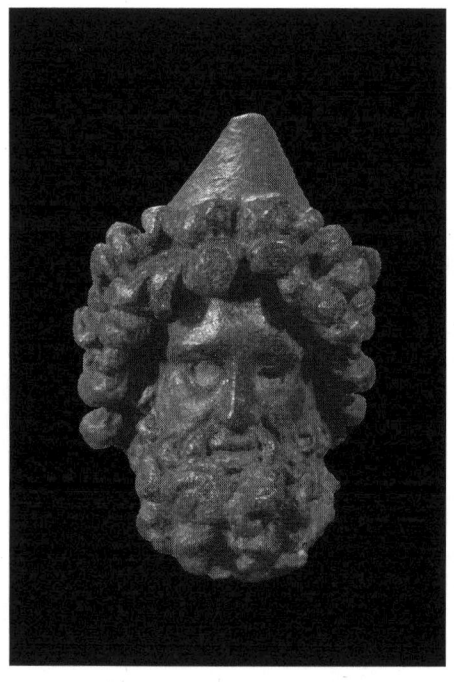

Copper alloy head of Vulcan, the Roman god of fire, volcanoes and blacksmithing. He was often worshipped in order to avoid destruction from fire

Roman

Believed to have been found in Cirencester

Accession Number C105

Awakening

SHARON WEBSTER

Recovered
from slumber,
a repose in Mother Earth,
its name triskele
And the swirls,
spirals that unfurl
with no end,
with no beginning,
confirmation of
allegiance
to an ancient world.
A time of words
that speak
of bravery and honour,
battles, valour.
The reward
lands of rolling hills,
of rain,
of green.
A trophy
for the Celts,
great glory
for the tribe
Dobunni.

The Forgotten Timepiece

ROSALIND NEWTON

Visits to museums have been important to me since I was a small child. They confront me with wonders not seen before, and lead me outside my world into that strange other country, the past.

I still like to stare in wonderment at the many artefacts that museums contain, in particular the Roman fragments and gold coins which have been unearthed from thousands of years before. They had their own fascination for me as a child, and in later years I was inspired to visit Pompei. The faces set in stone from medieval times also absorbed and scared me in childhood.

All those generations ago people were making things with tools which were rudimentary yet the craftsmanship was very often of high standard.

Those museum visits stimulated my love of history and set me thinking about time itself. As a child I would be urged by my mother, "Hurry up Sophie – you'll be late for school!" or hear as a teenager the impassioned pleas from my parents: "We haven't got all day. Get ready now – this minute!"

When I viewed the silver pocket watch all those years ago in the Corinium Museum dating from 1771 and inscribed *Francis Gibbs,* I was completely absorbed. I tried to imagine Mr Gibbs, whom I assumed to be a wealthy man, walking with a smart ebony cane and a tall black hat which he doffed when ladies passed him in the street. Perhaps he would take out the splendid watch on a chain that was nestling safely in his waistcoat in order to check the time if he was to attend a meeting or visit friends. I imagined Mr Gibbs' fingers touching the case as he gazed at the splendid dial. I also imagined the watchmaker, sometimes working in candlelight, totally engrossed in his work and feeling proud of his skills in fashioning such a watch. Expressions later came to mind involving time such as 'Time is of the essence', 'Time and tide wait for no man' plus 'There is no time like the present.'

Time marched on and I enjoyed visiting other museums at home and abroad. In the Cairo Museum, for example, I was again fascinated but disturbed to see mummified cats who had been placed in tombs with the Pharaohs who venerated a cat called Bastet.

After my father died, Mum asked me to come for the weekend in order to help her with some clearing out as she was thinking of moving to a much smaller home. It was an emotional experience for me sorting out items which had been gathering dust in the attic, including Dad's beloved train set. We were both grieving and it was tiring work. Cobwebs seemed to flourish in the attic! I had many bin bags of items to be taken to the charity shops. Dolls of many shapes and sizes from my childhood seemed to stare with reproach as I worked. Fluffy toy animals were tucked away with souvenirs from holidays taken many years before. One case was filled with my baby clothes – Mum had obviously longed for more children after me, but it was not to be. Old lamps, hats and walking sticks jostled with more suitcases. Very often I had to take clothes downstairs for Mum to check whether she wished to part with items for ever and there would be more tears whilst I waited patiently for her decision as to whether to part or keep them. I lost count of the times I ascended and descended the ladder linking the attic with the landing in order to confer with Mum who looked so frail and sad with more lines etched on her tired face. Old Father Time had not been kind to her over the years and especially since Dad's death.

On my last journey up there I spied a small box covered in dust, and tucked away in the corner of the attic. This had been hidden earlier from my clearing activity, so I took it down, after much sneezing, to show Mum as the box was filled with items carefully wrapped in very old newspapers.

There were some sepia photos in tarnished silver frames which we put aside to pore over later. At the bottom of the box there was a silver inkwell badly in need of a clean, and then I gasped as I unwrapped the very last item. It was a silver pocket watch! Memories were immediately rekindled of Mr Gibbs special watch seen at the Corinium! My hands were shaking as I held it. The inscription *J. A. Rowell 1871* was just visible on the back as it was very tarnished. The date was exactly a century after the watch inscribed 1771 in the museum.

I was speechless. There had been a special watch in our home and I never knew about it! Mum seemed very surprised too and initially was silent as she peered at the timepiece more closely.

'I have a vague recollection of your dad talking about a family watch but he thought it had been lost,' she murmured softly.

We talked long into the night and I found out, after Mum had checked papers in her desk, that my paternal Great Grandfather, was called John Alexander Rowell and the initials on the watch were his! Mum never realised that there had been such a special heirloom in the attic, and her lovely pale blue eyes filled with tears, as she pressed the watch back into my hands.

"For you my darling Sophie. You have your very own family timepiece now. Your Great Grandpa would be delighted for you to own it to pass on to future generations."

I married two years later and now have a baby son, John Alexander, named for his Great Great Grandfather. In due course the watch found in my parents' attic will be passed on to him. It is my sincere wish that he will cherish it too. Only time will tell. The memory of the silver pocket watch which originally belonged to Mr Gibbs still has a special place in my heart and my dear husband and I shall take John to see it in the Corinium Museum one day. I hope that museums will be important to our dear son. He may even decide to donate the family timepiece to a museum when he inherits it for others to enjoy. Museums are such special places which inspire a love of history, and in my case inspired the love of an heirloom, thought to be lost, and now found.

I remember the words of Paracelsus. *Time is a brisk wind, for each hour it brings something new.*

A fictional dedicatory tombstone inscription inspired by a grave marker at Corinium Museum

CHLOE HALL

To the spirits of the long departed,
Cynthia Verecunda lies here.
She lived for 27 years, four months and three days.
A beautiful, loyal, well deserving wife, four times
    a gentle mother.
Skilled with the lute, her voice was lovelier
    than a goddess's song. Snatched away suddenly she
    now rests in silence.
Guardian spirits, keep her safe.
Lucius, her saddened husband, had this memorial made.

A medieval birthing

MARGARET ROYALL

How brutal this birthing, upheld by her godsibbes,[1]
their presence essential, their touch reassuring.
Her labour is lengthy, a tight stomach grips her
in urgent contractions; fear gnaws at her bones.

The chair unforgiving, well-honed but so basic,
hewn out from an oak in an old English wood,
Adjustable ratchets and handles provided
to fit any wench, be she bonny or slim.

There is no adornment, no padding, no leather,
upholstered ones just for the privileged few
from well to-do families, the peasants must
suffer hard edges, steel rivets, an unyielding seat.[2]

Her godsibbes around her support her, they're caring,
give vocal encouragement, lifting her mood,
allaying her fears of a difficult labour

[1] *godsibbes* – birthing sisters. Middle-English word, later becoming gossips, as only women were involved and men were suspicious of their conversation.
[2] A medieval birthing chair was a highly uncomfortable chair made from wood, without upholstery of any kind. Sitting in it must have been excruciatingly painful.

and premature death giving birth to this bairn.

Now moaning and groaning she grips the chair's handles,
her features contorted by gut-wrenching pain
She sweats and then shivers, thinks not of her suffering,
but focusses hard on the child she must bear.

It's women's work, no man allowed to come near her
her young husband banned to the fields with his plough,
ears shut to her torment – the hours pass so slowly –
the process sheer torture, grotesque, inhumane.

He prays for deliverance, a live child with shrill cry,
its mother surviving the dangers of birth.
The long hours drag on, then at last they come running,
delighted, their message is one of great joy.

All well, she is resting: they have a new daughter,
a bonny young bairn with a sweet rosebud smile
and blue eyes, like his, that are sparkling with laughter –
He rushes to kiss her, his joy now complete.

The Passenger

ANDREW DONALDSON

You're smiling as you clamber onto the bus, a caress of the debit card against the reader, then a glance for empty seats as the accepted payment beeps behind you. It's late in autumn, where our daylight has been stolen and the burglary leaves us in darkness by 5pm. The stark white lamplights outside the museum moult into a warmer, but somehow less pleasing, yellow as you swing yourself into a window seat on the thankfully not especially empty bus.

The glow from the kiss is still on your cheeks, hairs on end, the thrill runs like a current that's charged you past capacity. You're full of a nervous energy that you should've walked off, a cocktail of adrenaline, excitement and hope shaken within a body in its early twenties. Home is only a thirty-minute walk, but getting the bus meant they waited with you at the stop outside the museum. A few more precious minutes of each other's company before going your separate ways. Them one way, you the other. Too early into the relationship to invite them back home. Maybe next date.

Your journey is swift. Two stops fly past uninterrupted by people wanting to get on. You'll be home too quickly for the buzz to have faded. You should've walked. You can't imagine getting home alone feeling this way – you'll never be able to sleep. You fumble with your phone and ponder sending a message but it's too soon. Too desperate. *They* have to message first.

You flip through your photos to pass time, smiling at the selfies you took together in the museum, while deleting the bad ones ruthlessly. You pause on the one in the medieval section, behind you a gargoyle's grotesque face and you both pulling equally disturbing faces between fits of laughter. A shiver plays on your flesh when you look closely at the face, a lolling tongue stretched out and two creepy small hands placed against each cheek. Lost in your bravado you'd leaned up and kissed it on the lips, ignorant of the *Do Not Touch* sign.

You sense someone beside you, which is odd because you don't remember the bus stopping or anyone getting on. You keep your eyes buried in your phone, oddly apprehensive of turning to look directly at this stranger. You raise your head and let your eyes dart around to take in the rest of the seats. There must be eight of them, all vacant. No, that is weird. Why wouldn't they have sat anywhere else? A light chill ruffles you, possibly from the open window, more likely from the icicle of unease that's forming.

Their breath is shallow. You can hear it catch in their sinuses, like steam through a clogged pipe. Internally you squirm, disgusted, but externally you hold it together. It brings back those memories of Covid where everyone was a threat, a walking infection. Everything tunes out as you focus only on this stranger beside you. This potential plague bearer who has chosen to sit next to you even though there are several empty double seats available. You wait on a cough, a sniffle, a something, an *anything* to force you to get up and move seats.

'Excuse me,' you hear yourself saying, you load the words into your throat like bullets, prepared to fire at the slightest sniff, but the figure gives away no sign of sickness other than their ragged nasal breath. Your words rust in the chamber.

Move anyway! You tell yourself but that twinge of doubt holds you back. A doubt that's your own social anxiety. Speaking in public is so much harder than typing it into a phone. You consider yourself an introvert but if someone looked at your social media, they'd laugh at that claim. Funny how you're so much bolder when there's no one to physically challenge you.

Through a combination of nerves and your own interpretation of the situation you do a mix of everything yet fulfil nothing. While shuffling in your seat, you lift an inch from your chair while finally emitting an almost mute 'Excuse me.' You cringe and curse your embarrassing, disobedient body, but maybe you can save it still. You've done enough to at least signal to the stranger that you'd like them to move. You steel yourself to stand up properly and get past them.

But they *don't* move.

Worse, they continue to face forward, and it's then that you really see their face. Its face. It's the gaunt roundness that shrieks 'unnatural' to you. Not horrifying, just hauntingly still. It has a dull complexion and sunken glassy eyes like a century-old porcelain doll; there are even tiny fissures in the cheeks where its thick foundation has cracked like weathered stone. It doesn't even acknowledge that you've spoken.

There are two or three stops left before yours. You need this person, this figure, to shift. You need to get away, to get out. You take another glance and this time you're sure that tiny lines have appeared around the corners of its mouth, there's now the hint of a grin. While not overt, you sense it's playing with you, taunting you. Is it daring you to try and get by?

Your phone dings, making you jolt in your seat. The figure next to you doesn't even budge, there is absolutely no give at all from its body. You try to push this thought from your head and go to look at your messages. It's from your date. *Had a lovely time. Can't wait to see you soon. Etc.* Earlier it would have meant the world, but right now you'll have to leave them on *read* until you're out of here.

Decision made; you move to stand up. Blood pumps into your quads as you prepare to push yourself up, but, as you rise, a tiny hand gently presses down on top of your right thigh, short stubby fingers curled tight around it. Its touch is cold but hard. You turn to look, but it still doesn't move its head. Those murky eyes stare dead ahead, and it's now when the panic takes hold. You realise you aren't looking at a person. This is no human being. It's the nightmare creature from the museum, that monstrous gargoyle. You lurch backwards, turning so the back of your head presses against the window just as the bus takes a sharp corner.

The horror beside you remains wordless but finally it starts to twist its head. Now revealed to you, you can see its ghastly face is symmetrical. The jagged grin splits the bottom third of its face almost in half and an impossibly long red tongue rolls out of its lips and whorls over its chin. Over the top of it all is its breath, its wretched stinking breath. It sounds as if there's a tear in its throat, a botched trichotomy patched up with masking tape.

Its fingers dig deeper into your thigh, the sharp crescents of its talons piercing the fabric and sinking into your soft flesh. You realise there won't be a next date; that there is no way out – that you will disappear. Your love will just think you've ghosted them and move on with their life; that the future of what you could have been will never dawn. A tear wells, a stinging wetness, and rouses you from your hopelessness. Your body revolts against the fears in your mind and, in that desperation, you kick out. The creature emits a phlegmy grunt as it's launched out of its seat and crunches onto the floor of the bus, its unnatural head cracking against the opposite row of seats. You're sure you see dust bloom into the air.

You hear cries from the other people but there's no time to think. This is your chance. You vault out, making sure you stomp down hard on the crumpled monstrosity flailing in the gangway as you sprint for the front exit.

'What the hell are you doing?' the driver yells, over the din of the screams and slams the bus to a halt. You leap up and bash the red emergency button that opens the doors and tumble out into the street. As your fist pounds the control you catch sight of the mirror that lets the driver check on his passengers. The shock of your own reflection overpowers everything else that you see. How your own face looks like it's made of stone, dusty and cracked. It's only when you're running full pelt home that your brain puts together that, in the mirror, the monster you'd sat beside looked like a vulnerable and broken old lady, and when you go to check for claw marks in your thigh there are none to be found.

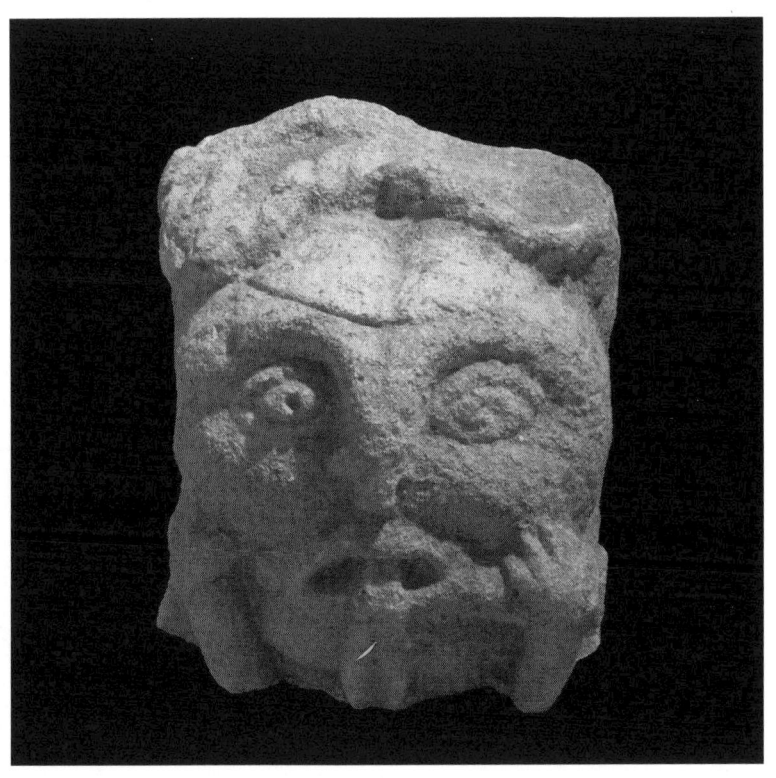

This medieval carved stone corbel is in the form of a grotesque head with its tongue sticking out. Grotesque carvings were part of the Church's way of communicating its stories and beliefs to a largely illiterate population

medieval

Accession Number G187

A lyrical retelling of Herodotus Histories, inspired by the Admiral's Walk Dolphin Mosaic panel

ARION AND THE DOLPHIN, RETOLD BY CHLOE HALL

Despite his youthful age, Arion of Methymna was the finest of lyre players and a singer whose voice always sounded divinely inspired. For some time he had resided at the court of Periander of Corinth. He felt warm gratitude for Periander's patronage and burgeoning friendship.

However, one day Arion was compelled by the gods to set sail for Italy and Sicily, to perform to local peoples there and increase his renown beyond the influence of the sun kissed Isthmian lands.

His tour passed off smoothly. Arion attracted many fond admirers. He also made a lucrative return for his virtuoso recitals. Each audience was emotionally swayed by his artistry. They compared his lyre playing to that of mighty Apollo himself. Arion realised the dangers of his newfound fame, and decided to return to Corinth from Tarentum, a crowning port of south west Apulia's inlet-studded coast. He soon fell in with a Corinthian crew whose vessel was shortly to set sail for their home port. His return to Corinth now seemed assured.

Yet Fortune was not feeling so certain. For soon after embarking on the voyage, those swarthy sailors quickly realised that Arion was carrying with him a telltale cloth sack. At once they plotted to steal his money. But to do so and remain undetected, they resolved to hurl their passenger overboard, far out at sea.

Arion became suspicious and a dream from the gods alerted him to the crew's deadly plot. Arion chose to plead for his life, and he threw himself at the mercy of the captain. He even offered the sailors all of the money he had earned. However, the sailors' cowardly fears for themselves prevented them from releasing Arion. Their cruel ultimatum rang in his ears: either he should take his own life, if he wished for a formal burial when the ship made landfall; otherwise he should immediately cast himself into the waves.

Arion begged one final request, after which he vowed to obey their command. When the captain learned that Arion wished to perform one final time, he readily agreed. Each crew member was also secretly pleased to have an opportunity to hear this famous musician.

For one last time, Arion dressed in his full costume and unhurriedly stood up on the half deck. He sang while accompanying himself on the lyre. The crew were enraptured by his talent. In spite of this, and as much as they admired his voice and playing, they simply looked away as he plunged headlong into the white crested ocean.

As the vessel sailed eastwards, into the blurring distance, Arion was flailing against the swollen currents. Embittered, his spirit was nonetheless accepting of his fate. Gradually his energy failed him. He called upon the gods with what he assumed were his final, broken breaths, appealing to the goddess Iustitia to avenge him. He closed his eyes and felt the waters closing over him.

Yet only moments later – fabulous to relate – the curving back of a lone dolphin broke through the tumbling surf. The noble creature presented itself to Arion with the gentlest flick of its greying tail. The musician understood what he had to do. With his final efforts he weakly clasped hold of the creature's sleek flanks and as it dipped, he was able to sit astride its glossy back.

While Arion clung on, the dolphin carved its smoothed route through the rocking seas, north eastwards towards Taenarum. Opened waters gave way to breezy, high cliff edges, which frowned over them a while. Then from beneath azure reefs peered up indifferently. Still the dolphin remained true and fulfilled its unspoken pledge to deliver exhausted Arion to shore.

Leaving him momentarily speechless too, on the rounded shingle above much gentler breakers, more ripples than waves, the dolphin clicked its own rhythmical farewell, then gracefully tumbled and rose into the renewing tide. Meanwhile Arion emerged onto the whitened sands, quite unharmed, though wearied to his bones. He looked around, observing as his saviour disappeared into the horizon, and cried out his endless gratitude.

He resolved to make his way overland to Corinth. It was a sun beaten route along ageless, rutted tracks, through high passes which plunged to the Spartan plain and twisted through gnarled, encroaching Peloponnesian woodlands. Ancient olive trees whispered to Arion on the summer's breeze – he must convince Periander of his miraculous plight.

Ten days later, following misty evenings and browning fields, Arion neared the clinging Isthmus, and so falteringly headed back into the court of Periander.

His host listened fair mindedly to the astonishing tale, but was almost immediately suspicious of Arion's most vivid storytelling. Periander needed to reconsider the threads of the knotted saga, and trace the treacherous crew. Therefore, again he kept Arion safely under the protecting roof of his home, until the sailors returned to that steepling harbour. Once they had nonchalantly moored up within the stone blanket of the sea's wall, Periander summoned them and asked after his long time house guest.

The sailors shifted uneasily throughout their interview. They glanced at one another. They could hardly admit what they had forced Arion to do. With nervous hesitation they swore in the names of the Olympians that Arion must still be lodging in Tarentum, savouring a break in his performances.

Periander grew increasingly tired of this deceitful web. Suddenly he clapped his impatient hands and reintroduced Arion to the betrayers. Glaring, Arion stood before them, wearing the same concert clothes in which he had plunged into the sea.

The crew were stunned to silence. How, they wondered, could Arion have survived? How even did he safely make landfall, and so eventually reach Corinth before them? The sailors had little choice, and through broken words grudgingly admitted their damning guilt.

Although the civic court was busy that summertime, Periander saw to it that the sailors felt the severe hand of wearied justice, while Arion became still more respected, but not this time on account of his musical talents.

A little bronze memorial statue was set up as a thank offering at Taenarum. The sculptor's labour featured Arion astride his dolphin, left in devotional gratitude to fickle Fortune and the all-seeing gods. Moreover, set into the porch floor of Neptune's temple, overlooking the wine dark Ionian Sea, was a simple albeit painstaking mosaic pavement, immortalising a tumbling, greying dolphin.

Sand Dollar

HILDA COCHRANE

In scuba gear we dived offshore,
a wreck in mind on seabed floor,
an artefact we could explore –
a relic of a distant age;

But we were wrong, it was not there,
an error, but we did not care …
deep down, white discs lay everywhere,
set on history's page

settled where sands rose to shore,
rolled by the tide on seabed floor,
restless roundels in their grave,
a diver's dream, treasure to save

Sand dollar shells, sea-songs of light,
vast bright profusion, pure delight,
we took them from that sunlit sea –
this treasure trove for free …

Then we left that glorious place …

our dollars, wrapped, and in a case
were taken from us, lost or thief …
Their fate was sealed without a trace,
and deep our dismal grief.

Hanging by a Horsehair

JULIE WILTSHIRE

The sword unearthed from the bowels of the Cotswolds
Is it the rusted Roman sword of Damacles?
In war and peace, we all have a spatha poised
    above our heads,
Our fragile lives, in imminent peril, hang by a horsehair.

Is it the rusted Roman sword of Damacles,
Above us, tempting fate?
Our fragile lives, in imminent peril, hang by a horsehair.
A moral parable, described by philosopher Cicero 45BC.

Above us, tempting fate,
History uncovers its secrets and repeats itself.
A moral parable, described by philosopher Cicero 45BC,
Makes us aware how precarious our existence is.

History uncovers its secrets and repeats itself.
The sword unearthed from the bowels of the Cotwolds,
Makes us aware how precarious our existence is.
In war and peace, we all have a spatha poised
    above our heads.

Herald

CHLOE HEADDON

They had both prayed to the gods for a boy: a son of Mars to bear the family name with pride and serve in the legion. They often walked to the temple in the heart of Corinium to place votive offerings upon Mars' shrine, wine and oil and, once, a tiny figurine of twin boys suckling from a she-wolf. At night they pressed their foreheads together, hands entwined, and though they both smiled with the radiant light of belief, their hearts whispered the truth.

When the girl was born, the mother wept: with relief, with exhaustion, with something else she could not name. As the midwife and the house slaves cleaned and swaddled the wailing infant, she strained forwards from the birthing chair to see, but there were too many bodies between her and her daughter, a maelstrom of female arms affording her the barest glimpse of that tiny, red body. It was only once the afterbirth had come and she too was cleaned, her sweat-soaked gown exchanged for a fresh silk tunic, her wild hair artfully pinned and perfumed, that she was allowed to repose on a bed and view her daughter fully for the first time: not as the baby was placed in her arms, but as the infant was laid carefully on the mosaic floor, squalling faintly. Too faintly. The mother barely dared to breathe as the father was let into the room, his urgent gaze finding hers at once. She had no need to tell him with her eyes; he'd already been informed of the sex before entering. He went to the baby, stood over her as she writhed and cried. He stared – with blank wonder or the impassive mask of duty, the mother could not say. Then a glorious smile broke upon his face. He scooped up their daughter and held her aloft, claiming her.

That night, they cradled their child in bed, the three of them alone at last. The girl would not be named until the eighth day – if she survived – so as they kissed her they only whispered, "Goodnight, sweet girl. We'll see you in the morning."

The child did not sleep well, that first long year. Her lungs, which had seemed too weak when she was born, found their strength in a piercing wail which resounded through the house, echoing from the painted walls. The wetnurse tended to her in a separate room, but still they could not rest while she was awake, and so they each took their turn to slip through the adjoining door from their bedchamber. They rocked and hushed her, tried to distract her by playing with the gold moon-shaped amulet around her little neck, turning it so that it blazed in the light of the oil lamps. They whispered to her stories of gods, heroes, and emperors in a distant land, so tired they scarcely knew which words left their lips – but it didn't matter, for the sound of their voices was like the flow of a river, bearing her towards slumber. When she finally quietened, the silence enclosed them like water, numbing, and they had to summon the wits to murmur, "Goodnight, sweet girl. We'll see you in the morning."

When she found her legs, she ran the house slaves ragged. *Little breeze,* they called her, for the speed at which she tottered between bath house and vestibule, atrium and dining room, or careered down the covered passageways where wool was dyed and linens were hung, as though wings sprouted from the tops of her hobnailed shoes. Her delighted laughter heralded her coming. She particularly loved the kitchen, where she always asked to be lifted up so she could see inside the lidded pot where the dormice were kept, transfixed by the little creatures scampering around the internal rings. Later, the chickens became her favourites. The mother often abandoned her meetings with the housekeeper, and the father his papers, when they heard flustered squawking in the courtyard. They smiled to watch their girl chase after the poor animals, or mimic the cockerel's puffed-up strut with her pudgy fists propped on her hips. Eventually one of the slaves let her help with collecting eggs, and from then on she became a daily presence at the coop, clumsily scattering grain and pulses for the birds and helping to refill their water dishes.

At night, she babbled before bed, no doubt telling her mother and father about all her adventures in incomprehensible child-speech, and they had to raise their voices over hers to say, "Goodnight, sweet girl. We'll see you in the morning."

The cough arrived like an ill-favoured houseguest slipping through the door. Her bright laugh quietened; her skin grew hot as though with inner flame. They laid her to bed and fed her warmed honey, but still her chest was racked with spasms. She howled with the pain of it, all the worse because she could not understand, and they wept too. The doctor they summoned suggested a tea infused with fenugreek; she squirmed and cried at the bitter taste no matter how hard they tried to disguise it, and it was only in those dreaded moments when she fell listless, exhausted, that they could spoon more into her slack mouth. Each night they whispered the words which had become their tradition – not as a promise anymore, but as a prayer. "Goodnight, sweet girl. We'll see you in the morning."

The mother placed coins, wine, and incense upon the shrine to their household gods; she ordered special cakes to be made, so that a portion might be given as an offering. The father sat through the night with their girl, listening to her desperate, shallow breaths. In, out, in, out, never enough. It was the sweetest of reliefs to hear the cockerel's first crow each morning, and see her dull eyes open and shine, just for a moment, the ghost of her laughter haunting the room. As much as he wished to, he dared not carry her outside to see her beloved birds for fear that even the slightest exertion would cost her too much, and so, after another unbearably long night, he brought her a gift instead.

The cockerel figurine had been destined to grace the upcoming festivities of Mercuralia in the temple half a day's ride from Corinium, near the great hill where the Dobunni had once held a fort. Finely wrought from bronze, its proud breast and wings brightly enamelled in patterns of vivid blue, red, and yellow, the cockerel was a treasure worthy of the god to whom the animal was sacred, and testament to his family's high standing – or so he had hoped. He could only imagine how the bronze would have gleamed, how those enamel feathers would have flashed like jewels in the firelight of the temple, as heady incense filled the air and worshippers hung Mercury's statue with wreaths of spring flowers.

As he revealed the figurine and gently perched it on his

daughter's chest, it wasn't awe which showed on her face. She grabbed the cockerel by the neck and brought its staring eyes closer to her own. Her small fingers probed the beak, which gaped as though caught in the act of crowing. She made what he thought was a squawking noise, if her lungs would allow such a thing, then an unmistakeable giggle bubbled out of her like water from a spring.

Funny. The cockerel was *funny*, and he saw now how the head thrust forwards gawkily, how the too-big, too-round eyes gave it a crazed expression, how the graceful curve of its body was completely at odds with the upright, startled jut of its tail feathers, wrought from a single disc of bronze, as though the wind had got up its behind. Gently taking the bird back, he made a show of parading it around on her little body, over her torso and up and down her arms and legs, pausing every now and then to mimic its cry and tilt it sideways, so that it seemed to look quizzically back into her raptured gaze.

As she fell into a slumber that seemed less fretful than before, he quietly fetched the mother from where she lay, herself exhausted, so that she might see the ease on their daughter's face. "Goodnight, sweet girl," they whispered, holding each other. "We'll see you in the morning."

The child's fever faded; she no longer gasped for every breath. When she was strong enough to get up and return to the daily life of the house, the cockerel went everywhere with her, its slim neck clasped tight in her fist. The only time she let it go was to feed the real chickens, because perhaps she did not want the animals to be jealous and think she loved them less. She walked, rather than ran, to their pen every morning. She talked quietly to them, calling them by unintelligible names she had invented. Gradually the father's guilt subsided over every hour he had to devote to his work, until his mind was full again of taxes owed and disputes in need of settling. The mother had her own preparations to occupy her; offerings needed to be made once more, rest taken, special foods prepared. Mercuralia passed, then a summer of endless, chill rain. Every now and then, they heard a desperate, high-pitched cough, and then they froze, skin prickling. The doctor was summoned back but offered no further remedy; the girl lived, he said. As often as they could, they consoled themselves by putting her to bed at the end of their busy days, the cockerel perched on the table beside her like a gleaming sentry. Her cheeks seemed rosy in the lamplight. "Goodnight, sweet girl," they murmured. "We'll see you in the morning."

The first they knew of sickness returning to their home was a slave complaining of a headache. The following day, the young woman could not work, her body was so full of ache and fever. One of the cooks grew ill next, then a young boy, then the girl who held the mother's mirror, until it seemed as though an invisible beast had swooped through the house, its dark, blighted wings brushing each of them in turn. They moved the girl into their own bedchamber, forbidding anyone else from entering. They burned incense constantly until her eyes streamed and her nose ran. They laid amulets on her chest, her brow, her tiny palms. They begged every god who might listen for protection.

The cough did not arrive slyly this time, but with a mule's kick that left the mother wracked with sobs. It consumed their girl; she was being consumed. The father reached for the cockerel, thinking to offer comfort, but his hand shook as though with palsy; he could not find the spark within him which had previously animated the bird. He sat, mute, beside his family. And when the coughing stopped, the silence was just as well, for the moment was unspeakable.

They buried her in the family plot just outside Corinium. She wore her hobnailed shoes. Into the casket they placed the cockerel, and while the gathered mourners nodded their heads sagely at the choice of companion, the father and mother, her belly swollen with a boy, could not speak to correct them even if they had the words. What use was it to call on Mercury to ferry the soul of their girl to the afterlife, when her place there was already assured? How could it be otherwise? Just as their hearts had told them the truth at the beginning, so it was at the end: their daughter already waited for them on the other side of that eternal sunrise, and the crow of the cockerel – *her* cockerel – would herald the moment when they were reunited at last. This was not goodbye, and so they told her, "Goodnight, sweet girl. We'll see you in the morning."

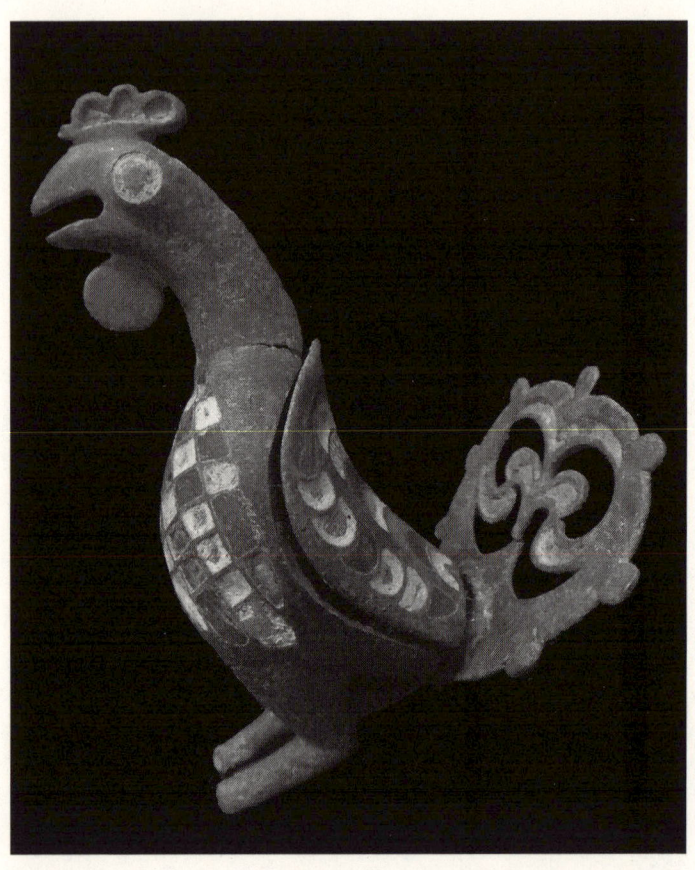

A rare 2nd century copper alloy cockerel figurine decorated with enamelled pieces found in an infant burial during excavations of the former Bridges Garage site, Cirencester. It may originally have been mounted on a pedestal, and it is also the only example that has the tail piece still attached. Cockerels are the patron animal of Mercury and one of his roles was to safely ferry the souls of the deceased to the afterlife

Roman

Accession Number 2014/42/93

The Horsehead Bracelet

VENETIA JOHANNES

Ashes, acrid smoke, grey tendrils twisting into the overcast sky. A dark symphony of greys and browns, as the burned out remains of the wattle-and-daub roundhouses gape, open mouthed in horror, at the sky. All that remain of a thriving community, those huts soon to return to the earth and sticks and shrubs that made them.

Scraping amongst the ashes, a flash of red catches the eye. The vermilion tunic beneath the Lorica Segmentata uniform of the Roman Legionary would always attract attention, and even more so amongst the dreary palette of the burned out settlement. A soldier scrapes through the last of the ashes in the hopes of booty. He has not had a good war so far, with booty unfairly shared amongst those of the right birth or cronies of the commander.

As he scrapes through with the butt of his spear, a flash glances off his dark eyes. Did he imagine it? No, there it was again, something in the centre of one of the burned out roundhouses. He approaches warily, not wanting to lose the glimmer. Rustling round in the sticky mass of grey and black ashes, still warm, he uncovers it: a silver torque, two horses heads at either end. For a few moments, he is struck dumb as he marvels at its beauty and craftmanship, the intricacy of the horses' heads, how accurate they are to life. Each tooth in the whinnying mouth, each strand of hair, each eyelash, is minutely detailed. Even then, they are slightly different. The muzzle slightly shorter on one, the lower lip heavier on the other, the ghost of a star on one forehead. Barbarians they may be, but the craftsmanship in metal and decoration of these Britons is second to none in the Empire. It is certainly not large enough for a man, possibly a child's or woman's.

A chill wind whips round through ruined village, funnels through the remains of the huts, kicking up gusts of stinking ash. Only now does the legionary notice the smell coming from the house he faces, the greasy, cloying stench of burned flesh. With a feeling of revulsion, he realises that the black chunks of ash are charred bones. He remembered, though for years he would try to forget, how one group of his legion was sent to round up those inhabitants good enough for slavery. The rest, the very old and very young, and the obstinate who would not bend to slavery, were barricaded in the houses, flames putting an end to their stories.

Cleaning the bracelet, he puts it in the small pouch he carries on his military belt. He will treasure this, keep it safe, and bring it home to the child he knows will await him back home. Perhaps he may still make her proud.

MANY YEARS LATER, the same overcast British sky overlooks a very different scene. A bustling settlement, centred on a newly built villa in the latest style, surrounded by all the buildings and features expected of such a noble residence. Barns, granaries, stables, luxurious gardens (one more expansive for leisure and exercise, others smaller and contained for vegetables and herbs for the kitchen or apothecary), a separate al fresco dining room for summer with beautiful views over the valley, a bathhouse, an extensive shrine to the local and empire-wide deities, and finally the slave quarters for the small army of stewards, maids, gardeners, cooks, bathhouse attendants, stable hands and other hangers on that keep it all running.

Near to the stables, the family to whom this villa belongs have gathered. They watch from a high wall that forms a natural viewing platform onto the riding ground below. There, a grey haired old man leads a young colt on a halter. They have spent many hours at this platform over the last few weeks, or so it seems to the *paterfamilias* – head of the household – as his daughter has insisted on watching the training process for her new horse. He has come a long way since he was a penniless legionary scrabbling in dust for booty. His dark eyes remain the same, and his upright military bearing will remain with him to the grave, now encased in a portly frame fostered by years of plentiful imported wine, local honey and prosperity. He has done well, and made a home in this land he once hated. He has done his best to Romanise it, as his comfortable surroundings attest.

The colt has been capricious, a chestnut firecracker pulled both by a desperate urge to please and a competing desire to assert its own will against the trainer. Today will be the first time she will ride him. The enigmatic old man is the villa's horse master, known for his great knowledge and years of experience with horses. His demeanour is unobtrusive, quiet, efficient. The perfect slave. On first meeting him few would realise that he is blind, unless he turns to the light, and the milky blue of his eyes reflects the sky and nothing else. He is one of the British slaves, and still insists on wearing the large moustache and clear shaven chin of his ancestors. His world revolves around the stables, his little room there, and the horses in his care. Few among the slaves remember what he was before, and he does not care to remind them.

He invites the daughter of the house down from the platform. The colt is saddled, expectant, waiting. The onlookers pause at their tasks, will the spirited horse accept the rider? Or will it throw her at the first test? Dressed in a short tunic and padded leggings, the girl steps onto a stone block and mounts the horse. It balks at first, but the horse master whispers soothing words in a language the girl cannot understand. She knows they are the language of the Britons, not their own language, and wonders if she should ask him to teach her some.

Throughout that afternoon before dinnertime, master, horse and rider go through their paces. The horse master has done well; the colt is biddable; the girl, happy; her father, content. As the sun makes its farewells and dips behind the sheltering hills on the western ridge above the villa, the girl dismounts and bids goodbye to her new horse, promising it the chance of a further ride tomorrow. As she leaves, she turns to the old horse master. A silver flash glances in her hand, as she removes a bracelet on her arm and hands it to the horse master. Before she gives it, she glances at her father, her eyes questioning, is this the right thing to do? A brief pause as his brows show the ghost of a frown, then a nod and encouraging smile. Yes, a fitting gift. Seeing his assent, the girl places the bracelet in the horse master's hands, whispering jumbled words of thanks and gratitude. He smiles, absently, feeling the unexpected object in his hands, lightly warm from the girl's arm. His fingers pause on the horses' heads.

THE TRAINING GROUND is almost empty. The family had left with their attendants, and the stable slaves did not need to show they were at their posts. Still, the horse master remains, fingering the bracelet in his hands. He knew that workmanship well, though it had been many years since he had last felt the curve of those familiar muzzles, the strands of hair so finely worked, those snarling teeth. It has been made by his brother, a master silversmith, in imitation two of his prize mounts. Made as a gift, for the birth of his daughter. In his mind's eye, he saw it now, sparkling on her arm in the sunlight as she rode her first horse.

He tried not to dwell on the past, it was best not to as a slave. To remember the time when he was a warrior, a chieftain, a leader of his people, when his eyes could see, only brought pain. That was before the invaders came, these Romanii, who fought in ways his people had never seen. Defeat, humiliation, slavery. He wished for death to end his shame, but then he still had some hope, perhaps he would bring some succour to his people by staying alive. He had had many sons, but only one daughter, the most precious of all. And the thought of her was what kept him alive too. For he lived with the hope that she too had escaped. She was of an age when the disaster happened that she would have been useful, no longer a young child, not yet a woman, the preferred age to take slaves and bend them to that life. The thought of her bound in slavery brought him pain, but he had reasoned that it always held the chance of freedom, not the finality of death. For all these years, he had lived with the hope that one day, he would see her again.

Haltingly, he picked his way back to his tiny room behind the stables. He knew things about this object that none still living could know. How the minute chip just off the centre on the ring was from where his daughter had unwisely thrown it around in play, and his regret at chastising her. How it reflected the shining coats of his horses as father and daughter admired his stables together, the finest in living memory their people had ever seen. How all admired her horsemanship from her earliest years, saying that she seemed an incarnation of the horse goddess Epona herself. How his daughter took that to heart, and created her own shrine to the goddess in their home, filled with toy horses, and carved an image of the bracelet above it. How every year his brother would increase its size, as her arm grew larger. How when his daughter reached womanhood, it would be reworked into an adult neck torque, a symbol of the protection her father would give her against all life could throw at her. How he had told her to never take it off, never give it up, never sell it, never lose it.

Only now, it would never grow larger. It would never become the woman's torque, just as his daughter would never become a woman. Feeling the familiar shapes in his hands, he knew with the sickening dread of certain intuition, that this had not been taken from her living. He saw now that the one hope that had kept him alive, to be with her again, rang false. Some confused thoughts turned to revenge, against the girl and her father, his owners, yet he felt so tired. He could not face the pain of creating more bloodshed. And his heart seemed to be beating very fast, his breathing laboured. He felt a scratching over his body, and realised he was sprawled on the straw spread across the floor of his little room. He could not get up. As he slipped, gratefully, into a deep sleep, he saw in his mind's eye the undulating hills above the villa, lands that were once his, overgrown with wheatgrass that billowed in the wind like a horse's mane at the gallop. Before him stood a beautiful woman on horseback. Her golden hair flowed down to the horse's hooves, her dress the same colour of the blue woad of his people, and of her laughing eyes. She wears a silver horsehead torque at her neck. Whether she was his daughter, or Epona, the guide of souls, he did not know. She stretched out her hand to him, inviting him to follow. He took it. When they found him a few hours later, his body was cold, the horsehead bracelet still in his hands. He was now with his daughter, and his gods.

Mosaic of the Seasons

CARLOS ALMONACID

Spring:
As the sun rises in the East, Flora springs forth
To bring life to flowers and trees.
As swallows fly through the skies,
They see rubies on the ground.
Flora's gift to her children.

Summer:
The sun's glow warms the earth, as Ceres harvests her crop.
To gather the grain, and bring it to her people.
Her sickle cuts through the long stalks, bringing down
    corn and flowers.
Her people are thankful, as the gift warms their hearts.
She dons her floral crown and smiles.

Autumn:
A dry season, as Pomona dons her leopard skin cloak.
She gathers grapes, ready for her people to devour.
She cuts through the darkening trees, wielding her knife
    with precision
Leaves fall in the breeze, as they turn red with age.
Pomona stares on.

Winter:
Missing, yet still present.
An emptiness as cold as ice, and as white as snow.
A hooded woman, wielding a bare branch
Who will remember?

Into the Iron Age ...
Life in a Roundhouse

CHARLOTTE PAYNE

I wake up to the sound of the cockerels crowing *(cock-a-doodle-doo)* then the geese calling *(Eeh Eeh)* and the hustle and bustle of the farm outside our door. I look out the door at the countryside and I say, "Godne mogen." (This means good morning)

Then I stand up. I pull my cow hide over my bed and I place my straw toys neatly on top (well, what stone age people called a bed; four pieces of wood upright with cow hides). Then I consider ... *what to wear? Ahh my favourite red striped tunic, I'll put that on. Ooof what a tight fit, I'll make a new one soon.*

Then my brother Corio runs over. "Keira, come on you're wasting daylight."

OK, that reminds me, I have to go to collect the milk for breakfast. Then I see the eggs sizzling on the fire in the centre of the roundhouse.

"Mmmm, eggs," I say. *No.* I tell myself, *snap out of it, eggs later, milk now.*

I get my sheepskin slippers and I walk outside. I go to Auro, our most trustworthy cow, for milk. I sit on the wooden stool and she ambles over to where I am waiting.

I get my wooden and bronze buckets and half an hour

later I have four buckets full of milk.

"Mum, I'm done," I say.

"Good, come inside for breakfast."

My eyes light up and I run as fast as I can with four full milk buckets.

I can smell the eggs, the meat, the honey and the bread, so I sit down and I dig in.

Ten minutes later, all that's left is a piece of meat.

"OK Keira, you're on the loom next," says Mum. (A loom is a piece of equipment for weaving)

I have to make a new flax tunic. (The fibres inside the flax plant were retrieved by rotting the stem of the plant in water filled pits and then spun in a similar way to wool)

Seven hours later …

"Done making and sewing it."

"Good," says Mum. "Can you come with me to collect berries?"

"On my way!"

I need my wooden basket so I pull it off our wooden table. I look on my berry chart as we walk. Mum made it for me so I don't poison myself accidentally.

At the end of the day Dad returns to our roundhouse with dinner: rabbits he has caught that afternoon. We devour them around the fire.

"Come on Keira. Eat up," says Dad. Later we all snuggle down on our beds next to the fire and fall asleep.

The end of our day living in a roundhouse.

Mourning

ROSAMUND BROWN

The vagueness of your Yorkist provenance provides hope;
the *may*s and *might*s evolve
while your blade seems to extend forever
in a glass shelf below;

on tiptoes
I can see right down
to your ghostly end;
a double handled sword,
one side paler, clouded, more unsure.
Both topped by a battered disc,
like a caved-in crown.

Your bright silver reflects me
thin, distorted,
like in a fairground mirror.
Beneath my twisted twin,
a scattering of claggy shapes;
Arrows for War.
A stuffed falcon hovers
ready.

The Painting

ALICE HART

Detectives Mary and Leon had been called in to investigate a robbery at the museum. One of the valuables the thief had left behind was a painting showing the local Abbey and the town streets. It was beautifully done, and the people were so detailed it almost seemed as if they would come alive at any moment. It was Mary who spotted fingerprints on the glass of the painting.

By then it was late, and Leon stayed behind to work on the painting, dusting it for prints after everyone else had left. As the door closed behind the last of the museum staff, Leon touched the painting, but immediately started trembling.

'W…what …?'

As he stuttered the words, the lights went out.

The next morning, Mary came in to look for her partner, but there was no sign of him, and the museum door had been left unlocked. The painting hung in its place, and Mary found herself drawn to touch it. As her fingers met the paint, the picture rippled as if she was falling through water, and then she blinked and found herself staring out of the glass and into the museum. She was inside the painting!

Mary forced herself to keep calm, and called out for her partner. 'Leon … Leon, are you here?'

All around, people walking the streets – the very same streets of the painting, the very same people in that painting

– stopped and turned to look at Mary. She stared back at them, unable to understand what she was seeing. Her mouth opened, but the question wouldn't come out. Eventually, a middle-aged man in a hat spoke to her.

'We got in the same way you did: by touching the painting.'

'But how do we get out?'

'Out? Some of us have been here for over two hundred years. Nobody gets out, and neither will you.'

'I will. I'll find my friend and then we'll leave together.' Mary ran down the street, calling Leon's name down the alleyways and into the shops lining the pavements, but there was no reply, and the other people just ignored her.

Finally, she gave up, and found herself wandering along with the other people, tramping the streets as they walked from one end of the painted street to the other, and then back again. Over and over, day after day, year after year.

Now I see your face, your eyes widening as you smile with delight at how realistic the people look. 'Mum, dad, come see this,' you call over your shoulder, and while you wait for them to arrive, you reach out and touch the painting.

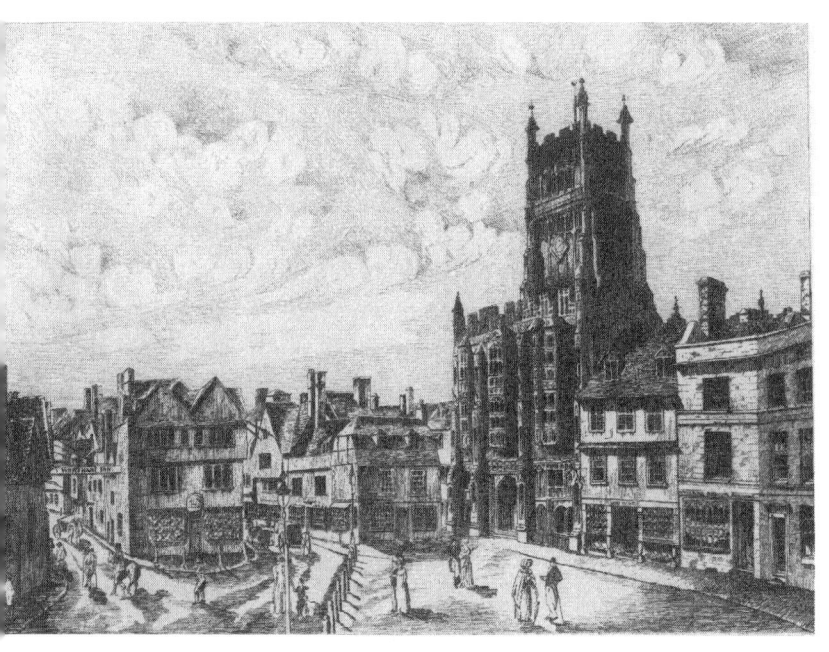

Engraving of the Market Place by J. Evans, 1805. This shows the Shambles and the shops, houses and lanes which had occupied the Market Place since the 13th century

Nineteenth century

Accession Number 2009/194

Out of Place

ANGELA REDDAWAY

I first met Mrs O'Brien when she turned up on my doorstep a few years ago. I had recently purchased a house in Suddington, a small, but busy town in the Cotswolds. In the course of sale negotiations, the previous owner had mentioned that should I need a cleaner, Mrs O'Brien had been 'doing' for her on a weekly basis for some years. I made no immediate decision about continuing the agreement but within days of moving in, she turned up on the doorstep, cleaning materials in bucket, ready to start. Judging from the ancient car parked outside and her own rather shabby appearance, I felt I shouldn't deprive her of what probably represented part of her weekly wage and I consented to continue the informal arrangement.

She did domestic chores for a couple of hours midweek, and we fell into an easy routine. I made myself scarce most of the time, but when she had a break, I would join her for a coffee and chat. During those early weeks, she proved herself very useful in supplying me with local knowledge about the shops and social activities in the town. The move had constituted a new start in my life both in terms of a new residence and my recently acquired status as a divorcee.

Mrs O'Brien was a gaunt woman, tall with a prominently-boned face, a slight squint in one eye – strabismus I think it's called – and large nose. Thin lips that gave her a severe look until she smiled, and then her whole face lit up and was permeated with kindness.

She talked animatedly, but without giving away much information about herself. Reluctant as she was to discuss her private life, I did deduce that she'd never married, neither had she any family still living. She regularly cleaned at several different locations which I assumed provided her with an adequate income. An erudite woman, Mrs O'Brien on several occasions, revealed herself to be knowledgeable about national and world affairs and I sometimes wondered why she had not chosen a more intellectual occupation.

One of her regular contracts was to clean the local museum located near the old railway station in the centre of the town. The artefacts contained there were dusted and cared for by the museum staff; their rarity and value would preclude handling by inexperienced hands. Mrs O'Brien cleaned the floor and the surrounding areas, office, kitchen, toilets and café.

'I love seeing all the displays, looking at the exhibits and imagining their history,' she told me once. 'It's such an interesting museum, with its Roman mosaics and Anglo-Saxon grave goods – so informative and such a diverse collection.'

She was keen to glean more information. One object, in particular, caught her attention. It was an oval piece of pale yellow marble, with a tiny engraving on the face. The size of a small lemon and oviform in shape. Closer inspection revealed difficulty in identifying whether the representation was human or animal. The miniscule face intricately carved, it's expression enigmatic. It carried with it a malignant aura, Mrs O'Brien said. No accompanying label to explain either its purpose or history, the object was displayed randomly among miscellaneous items. During one of our coffee breaks, I was treated to a detailed description made even more fearsome by the grimaces accompanying her squinting eye.

'I can't explain why I'm so taken with it,' she confided. 'It's such a mysterious little object, tactile but hideous. I find it very frightening and full of malevolence, yet I have this absurd desire to pick it up. I've never touched any of the pieces on display. I'd be terrified of breaking something.'

'It's a pity none of the museum staff are there when you clean.' Aiming to reassure her, I added, 'Perhaps you should ask them if you can take a closer look. They could probably tell you what it is.' The museum was mainly manned by volunteers and had restricted opening hours.

Mrs O'Brien didn't mention the item again during the following weeks and eventually I asked her if she had learnt any more about it.

'Oh,' she said shamefacedly, 'I don't know whether I should tell you. My curiosity got the better of me a week or two ago and I picked it up to examine it in more detail but I got such a weird sensation when I touched it.' She glanced at me cautiously, as if afraid I might laugh. 'I could feel movement in it, it was so uncanny. It almost felt alive yet it was icily cold and vile – I couldn't wait to return it to its place'

'Oh, you were probably afraid you'd be discovered with it in your hand,' I consoled her. "But I'm sure you were very careful."

'Maybe.' I could sense her reluctance. 'But the strangest thing happened. I distinctly remember putting it down again in exactly the same position, but when I got home that day, I found it in the bottom of my bag. I felt dreadful.'

'Of course you did. I expect you were worried someone might see that it had gone and blame you.'

'Well,' she agreed, 'naturally I would be horrified if anyone thought I would take something from the museum. I couldn't wait to put it back. I never heard any more about it. I don't think anyone had noticed it's absence.'

'I don't think anyone would suspect *you* of pilfering, Mrs O'Brien,' I countered.

She didn't seem very comforted by my words and I let the matter drop.

As the weeks passed, Mrs O'Brien became less communicative and rather morose. I began to wonder if I had offended her or she'd received some worrying news – about her health perhaps. She seemed so distracted that I felt I must broach the subject. To my surprise she started to cry.

'It's that wretched thing I found at the museum,' she struggled to get her breath. 'I can't get rid of it.' She seemed relieved to talk. 'It won't leave me alone. Each week before I leave the museum, I check that it's in the right place, but when I arrive home, I find it lurking in my bag.'

She looked at me pleadingly. 'Ever since it started happening, I've felt possessed by it. I know you'll think me silly but I feel as though it wishes me harm – I don't know what to do.' I was nonplussed. I have always regarded myself as not susceptible to anything hinting of the supernatural. Yet I knew Mrs O'Brien was not a fanciful person either, certainly not the type to entertain imaginative horrors.

I suggested that maybe she should talk to the curator and see if he could throw any light on the artefact's history, but she was concerned that he might doubt her integrity if she told him how the stone kept ending up in her possession.

The following week a grim-faced Mrs O'Brien undertook her usual cleaning routine at my house but was reluctant to talk further. The subject was obviously closed.

She got very distressed however, when she accidentally knocked over a figurine on my mantelpiece. Fortunately, it didn't break but she continued to berate herself for her clumsiness. As she left the house, she failed to see a wheelbarrow on the path and stumbled over it. Her knees were badly grazed but she rushed off before I could administer either comfort or first aid. I sensed that our amicable relationship was at an end, she seemed intent now on maintaining her distance.

A couple of days later I received a letter from her, informing me that she wished to terminate our cleaning arrangement. She blamed her deteriorating eyesight which was, she stated, affecting her vision considerably. She thanked me for my kindness but made no reference to the marble stone. I replied, thanking her for her service and offering any help I could in the matter of her worsening vision or in any other respect. I felt concerned and yet at a loss to know how to deal with the strange events that were obviously obsessing her. The idea that an inanimate object could exercise malignant influences was difficult for me to digest.

Life continued much as before, a young girl waiting to commence a degree course undertook my cleaning. I heard nothing more from Mrs O'Brien but thought of her occasionally and hoped the horror of the stone had resolved itself.

It was a shock, therefore, when one afternoon a

policewoman knocked at my door to tell me that Mrs O'Brien had been killed crossing a main road. The driver had told the police and ambulance driver that he was not driving fast and the woman he knocked down had seen him but continued to cross the road as if it were empty. He braked sharply but too late. Several witnesses had corroborated his account.

I was horrified by the news and explained that before she left my employment she had complained that her vision was worsening. The policewoman asked if I would identify Mrs O'Brien.

Surely there were friends or family that would do this, I protested. Apparently not. In her handbag she carried the letter that I had written offering any help I could give. In the absence of relatives or neighbours, the police hoped I would carry out the task of identifying her.

With racing heart, I accompanied the police to the mortuary. I was led through a series of corridors to a small room – the *Private* sign on the door barely hinting at the macabre task I was about to undertake. In trepidation I stood, knees like jelly, as the mortuary attendant pulled the curtain aside. He gently drew back the sheet covering the trolleyed corpse, exposing poor Mrs O'Brien. She looked even more gaunt and distressing in death. The length of her body was exaggerated by the severity of the white sheet covering her.

I felt deeply sorry, yet very afraid.

The attendant glanced enquiringly at me and I nodded. There was no doubt about the identity of the form before me. He indicated that he would leave the room so that I could pay my last respects in solitude. Desperately trying to overcome my growing sense of unease in the chilling atmosphere,

I stepped forward to express a silent and sorrowful farewell.

As I looked at her face, her right eye slipped open and revealed in the socket, a yellowish, engraved egg-shaped stone.

Survivor, Years Later

ROSE LENNARD

We fought hard and bravely, but what hope did we have?
They towered above us and came on us fast as flame.
Though our men were strong, no man on foot can outpace
a running horse, and our beasts, yoked to carts,
were lumbering. Many brothers died in the battle that day,
trampled into the good earth like dung.

Song thrush is calling the new day into being
as I thumb open my horse's mouth to sit the jointed bit
behind the big front teeth, in the gap our people
        never knew
could fit the key to mastery of such a beast,
the forged iron that would unlock such an alliance.
With grace he accepts the cold metal, lowers
his great head for me to part the heavy mane
around his ears, make space for the leather harness.
He nods is if to say *let's go*, pushes at me with his nose.

I ease onto his broad back, sit tall and gather up the reins.
We step through the dawn, the wind's hand brushes
the bowed heads of barley where my brothers fought
    and fell.
This is how the Romans would have seen our land,
stretched green below the hooves of steeds,
before the mud churned red with blood.
My horse knows nothing of this, his nostrils scent the air,
his furred ears swivel, his velvet eye looks to the horizon.

If the buried mouths of the dead whisper
from deep underground, this morning it is to say,
Life is sweet, brother! Touching my heels to
    the stallion's sides,
gladly he stretches his neck to race the running hare,
my hands steady on the reins, conduit to
    the iron bar resting
like tamed lightning on his tongue, ready for my command.
In the rising sun, I feast for the fallen ones.

Bradford Exchange

STUART SAMUEL

I had warm memories of that Sunday morning jaunt with my father when I was about thirteen or so years old. Church bells from Halifax Parish Church greeted us as we wandered down to the station on a bright spring morning, with the sun shining and birds singing, and, as far as I was concerned, without a care in the world.

We were heading for the train to Bradford, some eight miles away, which in those days of the early 1960s was formed of a newly introduced two-car diesel multiple unit. These were cleaner, swifter and more comfortable than the old carriages hauled by a bronchial steam locomotive. And, the biggest improvement of all, you could sit behind the driver, as on a bus, for the bulkheads of the coaches had glass screens through which you could observe the driver and the line ahead. At one end of the train, the front compartment was designated second-class – or *Standard* as it is now called – while at the other end it was first-class, and it was the luck of the draw as to which way the set was facing. We soon learned to slip in if it was first-class, for ticket inspectors were safely tucked up in their beds or digging their gardens on a Sunday morning and the guard was usually ensconced in his compartment reading the *News of the World*. The driver even sometimes opened the door in his screen for company and conversation with the passengers sitting behind him.

Those eight miles were filled with variety. Leaving Halifax station, with its all-pervading smell of warm toffee from the adjacent Mackintosh's factory, the train passed the junction to North Bridge and Queensbury, and alongside the flour mill into Beacon Hill tunnel, to emerge at Shibden Park with the swings and boating lake below. Then through the disused station of Hipperholme and into Lightcliffe tunnel, and round the bend to Lightcliffe station. The driver could speed-up on the straight stretch over the viaduct and past the site of Wyke and Norwood Green station, and into Wyke tunnel, followed very closely by New Furnace tunnel, emerging at the triangular junction with the line to Cleckheaton – with the over-flowing carriage sidings in the centre of the triangle – before stopping at Low Moor station.

This station had seen better days, with its four gas-lit through platforms and one bay. Next, the engine-spotters paradise – Low Moor Motive Power Depot on the left with its massive coaling-tower and engines being steamed ready for duty later. Then into the final tunnel on the route, Bowling tunnel, leading to Bowling Junction with the direct line to Leeds diverging to the right. I was always relieved to hear the woosh of air as the driver applied the brake for the descent into Bradford because the station was a terminal building, and sadly history has witnessed a couple of trains run away down this bank, with subsequent loss of life. So, eight miles of difficult line to engineer, and full of interest for a boy watching from the front end.

The destination, Bradford Exchange was a joint station, built by the Great Northern and Lancashire and Yorkshire Railways, boasting a magnificent double-arched roof spanning its ten platforms. It was a treasure trove of interesting nooks, crevices and buildings for a thirteen-year-old to investigate. There was a big signal box guarding the station throat, and wooden barriers with sentry-box type cabins for the comfort or otherwise of the ticket collectors. Through the barriers, my eyes were met by a large booking office and enquiry office, fully staffed even on a Sunday morning, a parcels office and left luggage office, a bookstall with intriguing reading material, and, very importantly, in the far corner, a refreshment room, to which we would retreat after a thorough exploration of the concourse.

Here my father would enjoy a cup of tea in a proper mug whilst I gurgled an orangey-type drink which had probably never seen the real thing, via a straw from a thin plastic container. And we'd share a Lyons Individual Fruit Pie – apple or blackcurrant flavour – shortcrust pastry with sugar on top, wrapped in its own box for the price of 6d.

But before the journey home, there was one further treat. In another corner of the station, next to the gentlemen's toilets, was a strange looking cast iron cabinet, fastened to the floor, and about 2ft wide and 2ft deep and 4ft high. The top surface sloped downwards towards the person standing by it, and there was a large brass-pointer, rather like a clock hand, which could be swung round like on a clockface to point to all the letters of the alphabet, numbers 0 to 9 and one or two symbols.

There were two levers to the right of the cabinet. Upon the insertion of 6d you could swing the clock hand round to the letter required, press the large lever downwards, and emboss a thin metal strip until you had composed the name you required. If you wished to emboss more than 12 letters you had to feed the machine more money. When satisfied, you pushed the other smaller lever downwards, which acted as a guillotine, cutting off the strip from the roll inside, and you collected it with excited anticipation from a tray at the front of the machine.

This machine provided endless entertainment during the journey home and at least the next twenty minutes as I admired my handiwork. My own name, embossed on a thin metal strip, for all my friends to admire. It also saved Father from wearing out his trouser pockets with all that loose change.

More recent googling reveals it was a BAC Nameplate Stamping Machine, BAC standing for The British Automatic Company Ltd of London. They were found on many mainline stations, and were, in a way, the forerunner of today's Dymo machines, but much larger and of course, far less mobile. Now, like the old Bradford Exchange station, they have disappeared – the embossing machine to museums and the station to a car park and the newly-built Bradford Law Courts.

The grammatically astute of you will remember I used the past tense in my opening sentence. For I later read somewhere that those embossing machines which had given so much pleasure to a thirteen-year-old had seen a more sombre use. Rather than children with their fathers playing with them, they were used by young men, called-up and bravely embarking upon a journey to northern France during the First World War. And the name tags were not for their amusement amongst their comrades, but kept about their persons for identification purposes were they to become one of the many pointlessly-slain on those battlefields.

With the mud and the squalor of the trenches of the Somme replacing the sweet spring morning in Halifax, the song of the birds being drowned by the noise of the battle and the carefree morning of the thirteen-year-old overtaken by the raw fear and futility of it all, I shudder as I recall I returned safely home to Sunday lunch with Mother from my adventure – a luxury many of those young men just a few years older than me did not enjoy.

Up close with China's Terracotta Warriors*

MARGARET ROYALL

We take our place in the snaking queue along
>   the museum walls;
the curious, the ancient history nerds, the Egyptomaniacs,
Excitement mounts.

We stare up at the clouds, as though they are the
>   ones in charge,
poised to blow the whistle, unleash a stampede into
>   the museum.
Anticipation rises to fever pitch.

Street buskers are staking their claim to the best spots,
>   hoping to
rake in the money, pounds, dollars or euros,
>   a lucrative prospect.
Music blares out.

At last the gates to antiquity creak open, a steward advises
>   orderly entry.
Like worshippers at a reliquary we nudge forward,
>   proffering tickets,
Synapses fire.

Once inside the inner sanctum we gasp,
    overwhelmed by the
reverence surrounding the lifelike warriors and
    180 artefacts on display.
Where to look first?

Our attention is drawn to a splendid chariot
    drawn by fierce stallions.
We can almost hear the pounding hooves,
    feel their steaming breath.
They are raring to go.

In each display there are gleaming jewels, gold horse
    fittings, ritual items
including a huge bronze cauldron to accompany
    the 1st Chinese Emperor
into the afterlife.

We are overawed by the insights into this ancient culture,
    the audio-visual
material bringing to life this rich heritage, seamlessly
    linking ancient to modern.
We hold the memories, cherish them deep within.

---

* Memories of visiting Liverpool's *World Museum 2018* for the exhibition *China's First Emperor and the Terracotta Warriors.*

An Ode to an Iron Age brooch, excavated at Kingscote

STILL CLASPED, BY CHLOE HALL

O ancient copper brooch pin, olive brown from
    timeless years,
Did your trusted clasp once tightly grip a Celtic birrus?
You're beyond an inspiring, decorative souvenir.
We know how you were cherished, and still your smoothed
    form cheers us.

More striking than a button, or metallic fastening,
Did you embellish status, did you match a signet ring?
Still your pin's point snugly rests in its catching plate, arcing
To your moulded bow, blemish free, a perfect tethering.

I wonder, who was the last, the very last Celt to bind
Her winter's cloak or summer's dress folds with you,
    fine brooch pin?
Was she a young mother, whose children occupied
    her mind,
Or an older clanswoman, long respected by her kin?

If only you could let us know, we have so much to ask
Of ancient secrets you have seen, dark times,
    and brighter past.
As farmers toiled in their fields, you were steadfast
    in your task –
Through grateful hands of unknown generations
    you have passed.

There must have been one final time when thankful
    fingers flicked
Your clasping form to release some familiar textile.
What happened next? Your owner's passing?
    A local conflict?
Or did Rome's hobnailed boots drive your people into exile?

After fifteen hundred years you were unearthed
    at Kingscote's
Roman town. Perhaps a legionary stole you, as he
Burned your roundhouse down. Or did a travelling
    merchant gloat
When he traded you? Or did you keep his family free?

We may never find the answers to solve your mysteries,
But surely that's one reason why we feel so drawn to you?
A Celtic blacksmith's skill, besides your unknown history,
Means you'll keep riveting our curiosity anew.

Bird Brooch

JULIE WILTSHIRE

Released from captivity,
From a Cirencester cage.
A prisoner bird acquires,
Its belief in its own immortality.

The once lost amphitheatre bird,
Ruffles its enamelled crimson wings,
In preparation to take flight and flee,
Into Heaven's brocaded tapestry.

Zoomorphic brooch,
In Roman times,
Did you clasp a heavy heart,
Weighted down with doubts?

Were you a precious gift,
Given with love,
Then cast idly aside,
Like a rose that had wilted and died?

Beneath the flower filled fields you lay,
Until history triumphed over time.
And from the tomb of the earth,
We rejoiced in your rebirth.

When the world in its innocence sleeps,
And dark agents stealthily creep,
Shine dear bird like our morning light,
Amongst the arrival of the witching night.

With the beating of your wings,
O wondrous work of art.
Fly in freedom, fly,
Amongst the star strewn sky.

In the museum's conspiracy of silence,
Amongst the antiquities which escaped time.
The sweetest note can be heard,
From the awakening beauteous bird.

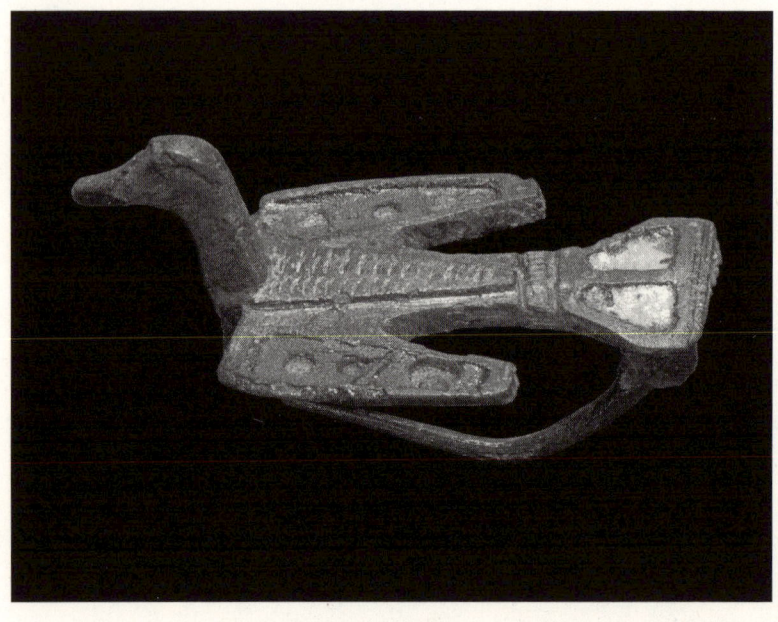

Copper alloy zoomorphic bird brooch decorated with blue and red enamel. Many different types of brooch were worn as a way of fastening clothes. Zoomorphic brooches were very popular; other animal shapes encountered include hounds, hares and stags. This brooch was found at the amphitheatre, Cirencester

Roman

Accession Number 1980/62/415

Sleeping Cavalry

REBECCA MCDOWALL

The two soldiers sat under a thicket of trees at the outskirts of Corinium. Their horses carefully tied up behind them lazily grazed. The trees provided a welcome reprieve from the relentless sun that had been beating down on them all day. It wouldn't be long before they would have to make their way towards the Basilica, their entire calvary unit were to be there tonight. With the Senator visiting, it would be on their heads to ensure his visit went without a hiccup.

Maximus withdrew a folded square of fabric from his saddle bag and started to methodically wipe down his spatha. The sword had served him well over the last few years, all who had stood in his way had been swiftly felled. There was a price for disrupting the Pax Romana. One he was proud to enforce. He examined his already clean blade, before starting again. Wiping away non-existent stains. It was a routine he found himself falling into every dinner time. He knew that other than the sweat that had soaked through his uniform, he was spotless. But he couldn't eat. Not until he had rubbed off every stain.

Quintus on the other hand never seemed to have much trouble with sitting down to eat. Maximus cast an eye over him. Quintus was new to the calvary this year, and therefore his responsibility for the time being. As the new recruit sat on the moss covered log, slowly eating porridge from his copper bowl, he couldn't help but wonder how Quintus could simply switch off so easily. It was a question that would never leave his lips. He would never provide the fuel for his position in the calvary to be questioned.

"Wine?" Quintus called over, as he walked over to the saddle bags in search of some.

"Indeed." One would not hurt before they made their way back into the town. Afterall he was not a man who enjoyed drowning in his cups. Yet he welcomed the bitter bite of the raw wine.

As he sheathed his spatha, he glanced once more towards the town. His lids weighing heavily in the oppressive summer heat. Surely the unit would not miss him. The Senator wouldn't notice, of that he was certain. The pressing urge to sleep demanded his attention. Maximus lay his head on the saddlebag. Perhaps the wine was stronger than usual. Sleep would solve it. He hadn't noticed Quintus unconscious face down in the summer grass, next to the horses. His cup long forgotten about, the dregs leaking into the earth underneath.

Maximus laughed deeply to himself convinced he must be dreaming already as the lilt of soft voices from the thicket reached his ears.

"How much Valerian root did you mix in their wine Augusta?" The older voice sounded as if she was scolding the first.

"You worry too much Hadrianna!" The lilt of the first voice drifted back. Maximus was curious to whom it belonged to, but he no longer had any desire to try to open his eyes.

"I had the new herbalist from the market, Fausta, mix the

concoction for me. It won't do these two any harm. They'll just enjoy a peaceful slumber for at least another day. They shouldn't give us any trouble now".

The two women observed the sleeping soldiers for a moment more through the tree branches until they were satisfied the valerian root had done its job.

Approaching warily, each held a roughly spun sack in their hand.

"Quickly now, pop it over his head. Not too tight though!" Hadrianna whispered briskly as she threw her sack over Quintus's head.

"Why do you think they want these two?" Hadrianna couldn't help herself. She had been wondering ever since the cloaked man had arrived at her doorstep two nights previously with a purse full of coins.

"Shush. It's not our job to know. We just have to make sure they are out of action for a while. Now help me untie these horses. The men will be here soon to pick up those two." She gestured towards where the two soldiers now lay bagged up behind her, sleeping peacefully, oblivious to the peril they had been caught in.

The two women made quick work with the horses, carefully removing both saddles and bridles. They were beautiful creatures. Augusta longed to take one back with her, but too many questions would be asked. She ran her pale fingers through the chestnut horse's mane.

"Now go" she murmured to the horse. "You get as far as you can from here." She patted its neck one more time before lightly swatting its flanks. "Get out of here."

"I'd tell you to drink some of their wine, but a fat lot

good that will do you." huffed Hadiranna as she piled up the soldiers' weaponry next to the spilt dinner bowls. "Leave it there. Someone will find it eventually."

The Ammonite

MARY MOORE

It came as part of a load.
The newly refreshed drive
Was its new bed.

Mottled and brown, it lay
Among the myriad offerings
From the quarry.

But, how long had it lain,
Unknown, unknowing,
Lost in the earth's silence?

Only the sound of the sea
Rang in its ears
Until the clamour,

The roar of a new thunder,
Not waves, but shovels,
Broke in, clamouring

Around its silent
Resting place.
And it found me.

The Time Keeper

JONATHAN HART

He had to possess it. Lewin stared at the face peering back at him through the glass. Ivory rimmed with gold, Roman numerals dividing day and night, the hands still and silent, as if waiting to mark time, to count down a life.

He'd come to the museum in desperation, seeking inspiration for his long overdue tenth novel, but now all thoughts of his agent were forgotten in his desire to own the pocket watch. *Emanatists*, it read, in the place of the maker's name. Words and names were Lewin's trade, and so he knew that this watch, with its curious name, was rightfully his.

In the end, it was easy. The cabinet was old, barely fastened, and it was the work of moments to slip the watch into the breast pocket of his jacket. Its weight was comforting, and he could have sworn the mechanism started ticking the moment it pressed against his heart.

The stories came easily after that, but though they filled Lewin's head, he found no time to bring them to life. Instead, he would gaze lovingly at the watch, fascinated by the traverse of its hands. Minutes, seconds, hours became days, weeks, months. His phone stopped ringing; friends ceased to knock at his door. Perhaps he ate, but, if so, he had no memory of it.

People would avoid him on the street after that, a bearded, gaunt man who muttered to himself. Some of the kinder ones tossed him a few coins, or bought him a coffee, but he'd only glance up at them, his eyes full of cunning, before returning his attention to whatever he had secreted in his jacket. A drug of some sort, they thought.

Then, one day, Lewin was shuffling past a street corner when a small shop caught his eye. The outside world rarely impinged on his life, but here was a flicker of memory, a street that had featured in one of his early stories. This shop had not been there then. He had no recollection of it, and so he pulled his attention away from the watch, and gazed instead through the curving glass windows, seeing an array of antique jewellery, some of it unfashionably heavy and Victorian, other treasures crafted with the daring lines of the twenties and seventies, and yet others far more ancient.

Curious, he stepped inside, hoping the owner might be able to tell him something about his watch.

The shop was small and dark, lit only by candles, and yet filled with more glittering cabinets and heavy mahogany drawers than should have been possible. At the far end was a wooden counter, and behind it stood a dark-haired woman so flawless that she might have been crafted by some master jeweller herself.

An onlooker, had there been one, might have expected her to press a panic button upon finding this stinking, grimy man dragging himself into her gleaming shop, but the woman smiled at Lewin as if he was her most valued customer, a man able to meet any price. She watched him hesitate as he reached into his jacket, his fingers caressing the smooth casing of the watch, feeling its warmth penetrating his skin as if it were a living thing. Slowly, as if he couldn't help himself, Lewin drew the object out, holding it towards the dark-haired woman, allowing it to catch the dim light.

'A fine example.' The woman's voice was smooth, her accent unplaceable. 'Do you wish to sell it?'

Lewin stepped back, glaring at her, 'Never!'

The woman held up her hand, soothing the atmosphere, her motion arresting Lewin as he started to shove the watch back into his pocket.

'I assure you, I would never wish to force a trade, but if you want to, if you truly want to, then you will find my offer very competitive.'

'MINE.'

The woman gave a slight shrug. 'As you will. You look hungry though. Think what you could have, what I could give you. That watch is such a small thing to you, but to me — well I would give you whatever your heart desires.'

Her eyes held Lewin's, blue eyes so pale it was as if time had drained from them and she was speaking to him from across an eternal abyss.

Lewin's stomach growled noisily, and all at once he realised how tired, how desperately exhausted, he was. He longed for nothing more than to lie down right there on the floor and curl into a ball, to sleep and sleep and sleep, and then to wake up and for the stories to come. He wanted to be back where he'd been before the watch: a successful writer, hungry for his next great story.

Lewin held the watch towards her. 'Whatever I want?'

The woman's eyes glittered. 'I know you, Lewin Armstrong, writer of ghost stories. Your ideas made you a wealthy man, did they not? Yet now they dance away from you, forever just beyond reach. I can change that. Money, fame, adulation. You'll have it all, my sweet one.'

Now he was pressing the watch into her hand. Her alabaster fingers closed around the case in a way that suggested familiarity.

The woman pushed a sheet of expensive looking paper towards him. 'This is the bill of sale. I'll need your signature at the bottom.' She offered Lewin a fountain pen and watched closely as he signed his name. 'It is done.' There was hint of triumph in the curl of her lips.

'My stories — you'll give me ideas? Email them to me?'

'As I said, Lewin Armstrong, it is done. Write, share your thoughts. I promise you'll have fame beyond your wildest imaginings. Isn't that what you want, my darling precious — for people to love you, for all those who doubted you to admit they were wrong?'

He smiled. Happiness flooded his mind, and with it came a surge of ideas, cascading over one another in great roller coaster waves. He hurried towards the door, desperate to write them down.

As Lewin grasped the brass door handle, he paused, turning back to the woman. She was still there, watching him from behind the counter, her eyes shining in the candlelight.

'The inscription on the watch face — a maker's name, I assume?'

She arched an eyebrow. '*Emanatists*. A very rare mark. The only one of its kind ever created, in fact.'

Lewin's face fell. Had he been duped? What had this woman actually given him in return for this unique object, something that collectors would surely pay handsomely for?

The woman held the watch up, tilting it so that the case reflected the flames. 'Emanatists,' she repeated. 'It's not a name, it's a word, but I'm sure a writer as great as yourself knows that.'

'I do, of course. I just can't recall its meaning.' Lewin flushed with the lie, glad of the dark.

'It means those who believe that the universe has a creator.'

'Oh.' Lewin shrugged. There was nothing special about the word, just some religious motif added at the request of its original owner.

The woman smiled, her teeth showing very white against her lips. 'Words have power, my sweet, but you know that being a writer. The power to entertain, to make people love, to make them laugh, make them cry. The power to bind. Rearrange the letters of a word, and you change its power.'

Lewin frowned.

'Oh, come, dear, sweet Lewin, you who love wordplay so much in your novels. The misconstrued love letter, the poorly crafted suicide note. Emanatists. Take the letters, play with them, amaze me with your acumen.'

Lewin stood in the door, his lips moving as letters skittered to and fro before his eyes. A, N and S coalesced. His lips moved more, mumbling. The sound joined the ticking of the clock. 'Time,' he murmured, 'time.' His lips continued to mouth as letters slotted themselves into place, and then he raised his eyes to meet those of the woman.

Her lips curled in a leer as she ran her fingers over the watch, stroking its case. She nodded. 'You guessed it in one, my clever little magpie. Emanatists becomes two words.'

Satan's Time. Lewin's eyes were filled with dread, but those of the woman gleamed.

'Sweet writer, I shall enjoy watching the seconds of your life ticking away. Now go, write those stories, thrill your eager readers.'

Lewin flung the door open, stumbling on the mat in his haste to leave. Just before he closed the door, the woman called after him, 'Be seeing you.'

Then she took the bill of sale with Lewin's signature and placed it within a thick ledger. Against her breast, the pocket watch ticked patiently.

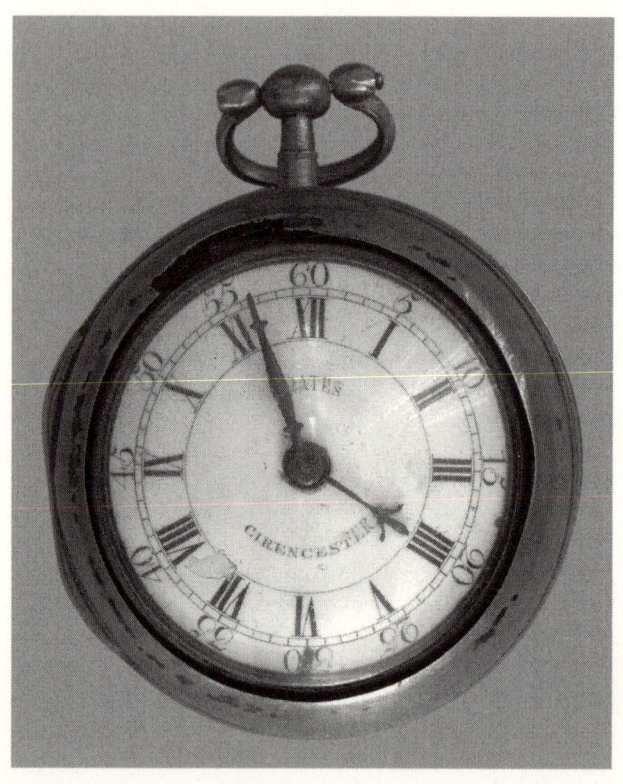

A cased silver pocket watch made by Coates of Cirencester, a maker noted for the high quality of his workmanship. Coates appears to have had premises in Dyer Street, Cirencester. The case is inscribed with the owner's name, Francis Gibbs, and the date, 1771

Eighteenth century

Accession Number 2004/33

Genus: Museum

ROSAMUND BROWN

I love your dimmed down-lights on muted carpets,
like the hushed entrance to a cinema screen,
or a plush, soft-lit charnel house
open for a special viewing of bones;
unknown trephined skulls,
mock Anglo-Saxon burials,
a mammoth's tusk, a femur.

I love your Roman brooches,
your decorated games' tokens,
your Viking drinking vessels,
your tegulae, your civil war muskets,
your Victorian bonnets,
your canopic jars,
your stethoscopes, your tongue scrapers, your glass syringes,
your discoveries, your sadness.

I love your reconstructed medieval streets,
your crowd sounds from an often-broken speaker,
your sewer stench,
your smell boxes;
carbolic, lavender, and musty clove,
fumes like church, but more of a sanctuary.
Your coolness in summer,
your constant, comforting format,
spliced with your evolution.

I love your marble phalluses,
and the broken stumps,
your trilobites, your geodes, my lithic love.
I love deciding I am more bonobo than chimp,
as I rifle through the dressing-up,
settle on a Darwin beard.

I love your hoards, your hordes;
the mooch, the silent slow dance
with other lovers,
as we pass to exchange spots
in front of staged spilt coins.

I love your glossy guides,
your tanned typed cards,
your laminated pages,
your lift-the-flaps.
I love your headless mannequins,
your reenactors,
your verbose volunteers,
your tantalising store room doors,
your over-priced gift shop.

I love that you map your nervous system
across the whole country,
covering tiny towns and big cities.
Stretching out over oceans,
feeling for the familiar, and the new;
connecting with all the beautiful bright shapes
on this delicate antique globe.

Mē paenitet

VICKI FLETCHER

Digitising the collections was taking a long time and Amber yawned as she slid open yet another drawer to uncover the object within, nestled in tissue paper with a paper ID that had no doubt been written decades ago. It was a good thing everything was being updated, she thought, squinting as she attempted to read the cursive, before giving up and focusing on the object instead.

It was a single earring, simple in its design by modern standards but undoubtedly the height of fashion when it was crafted, some two thousand years ago. A Roman earring, gold and turquoise with a single pearl, it held a quiet, sombre beauty that made Amber's breath catch in her throat. The woman who had worn this – this one item she probably had no concept would outlast her civilization – was long since gone from this world, and the world she had inhabited.

Amber knew that if that woman, whoever she had been, were to see the world of today, she never would have believed her eyes. And yet, while everything had changed, nothing had.

In place of cobblestone roads and carts were tarmac and cars; rather than raucous amphitheatre shows, the latest movie in dim cinemas. Fast food and cafes had replaced their ancient counterparts, offering coffee and burgers instead of spiced sausage and wine, while gambling and dice stood the test of time.

The thought made Amber feel close to this woman; the owner of this earring. With a gloved hand she gently touched the artefact, lifting it from its tissue paper, and at once a rush of sounds, smells, and sights overtook her. The museum was gone. Instead, Amber stood in a busy street with stone and timber buildings lining the sides. People bustled, but not the people of her time; these wore linen and wool, togas, tunics and fringed stola. Instead of Doc Martens and trainers, leather sandals and slippers padded along the stone pavements and the language being shouted by vendors was familiar and yet alien, half-remembered from Latin lessons many years past.

She cast her eyes upwards. The sky, blue and slightly clouded, had no planes and no vapour trails belying their existence. Birds chirped and the town bustled, and tears sprang to Amber's eyes. She took a step, then another, and before long she was racing through the streets, dodging Roman men and women, slaves, artisans, actors, vendors and prostitutes. The scents were full, the sights bright. The buildings shone, new and resplendent, ignorant of their future as fragmented remnants below the ground.

She emerged from the side roads on to the main thoroughfare – was this the forum? – and, panting, looked left and then right. The road continued, straight as an arrow, to gates in the walls; walls she knew would surround the whole town. Vicus, she corrected, giddily.

The larger gate caught her attention. Verulamium Gate, she thought. It led to Londinium – the gateway to the rest of the Roman world. The urge to walk that way, to follow the road and allow her feet to take her across the country, along the straight road to London and on to Rome itself, was overwhelming, and she almost gave in, taking an almost subconscious step when someone bumped into her, knocking her out of her reverie.

'Mē paenitet,' apologised the woman who had bumped her and Amber almost responded before shaking her head and simply smiling, not remembering how to respond in Latin. The woman nodded and turned away, and as her head swung the sunlight caught on her jewellery, flashing gold, and turquoise, and pearl.

Amber's hand tightened. She still wore her gloves, and still clutched the earring in her hand – an earring that looked worn and degraded compared to its past self, resplendent on its owner's ear. The woman walked away, earrings swinging with every step, and Amber watched with a smile on her face and a tight feeling in her stomach.

The woman was about her height, with dark eyes and brown hair much like her own. She was about thirty, the same as she, and while Amber had no idea how her own life would end, she knew, vaguely, what would happen to this woman. Her way of life would last a couple hundred years more and then crumble away, leaving the trappings of her town hidden beneath the soil for curious archaeologists to discover nearly two millennia later. Her home, her belongings – all of it would fade until no evidence of her life remained. But not her earring. By chance, this one piece of jewellery, fallen perhaps from her earlobe as she shopped, would somehow remain and be found where it had dropped, winding up in a tissue-lined drawer in the local museum, to be loved and marvelled over by people who would never know its owner's name.

She almost followed her, chased after the woman to make it right – to be able to tell the future, this earring belonged to this someone – but as she stepped forward the world shifted once more, colours muting and sounds fading, until she found herself again in the collections room of the museum, the archives laid out before her and the earring laying gently in the palm of her outstretched hand.

She remained silent, still, for a moment, and then carefully returned the earring to its resting place. She closed the drawer, the smell of spiced sausage and horse manure fresh in her nose, and stripped her gloves off. As she switched off the lights and left the room, leaving the artefacts to sit in the darkness they had become accustomed to, she swore she would make sure the earring found pride of place in an exhibit soon, perhaps along with a drawing of the woman who had once worn it.

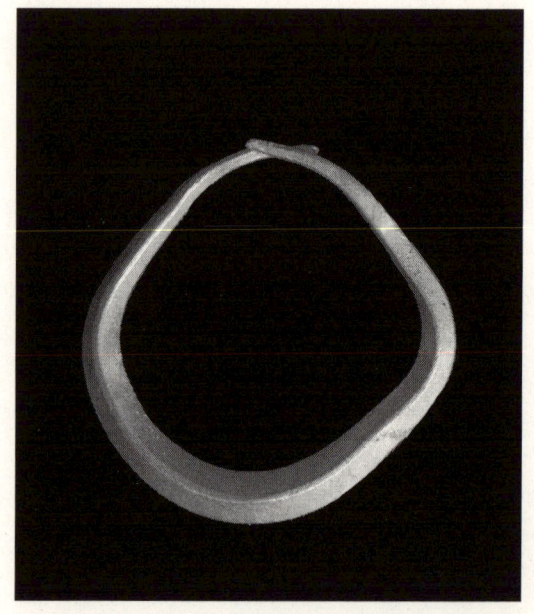

A Roman gold annular earring. Found at Long Newnton, Tetbury

Roman

Accession Number 2014/8

Epistle to Sir Robert Atkyns

GRAHAM POWELL

This morning to the town of which you spoke
To view the noble landscape and its folk
Of whom I met a number and their esquire
Bathurst, with whom full well I did enquire
How I might make majestic his estate
For those to view at some far distant date.

His reputation when his time has passed
Was all he craved unto the very last.
The while we talked o'er the manner of my craft
He asked, if I *might discomfort*, so he laughed,
The temper of *a lesser squire* than he
And how he would redouble then my fee.

The gardens of the Abbey House nearby
Are masterful and pleasing to the eye
But them I *could diminish and reduce*
And make them, next to Bathurst's, *more obtuse*.

This, *Allen*, as he said that I should call him
Is a man of subtle wiles and sturdy limb,
Of much ambition and of vaunting wealth
And, so it seems, inclined to act by stealth.

Walking from out the town a mile or so
I came upon a tump, a long barrow
And there sat down the better to survey
An elevated vista and assay
How best I might present the place with all
Its ancient charm: the church and merchants' hall,
The market, shambles, parterres, orchards too
And inns whose signs I saw, more than a few.

I will with license manicure the scene
Divert the Churn and cause all roads to lean
Towards the stately home and its estate
(Our squire, past doubt, ennobled at a later date)
A scattering of trees, formal gardens laid,
Orchards full in leaf and ev'ry lane well made,
No taint of ordure nor signs of ugly strife.
Nothing to cast aspersions on his life.

And yet, despite the present urgings of this gent,
Some time and purpose will by me be spent
On the etching of a plate to celebrate
The Abbey and its grounds that I, in truth, would rate
Much finer and aligned to future taste,
When Bathurst's parkland has been laid to waste.

Once etched two copies soon to you I'll send
Your obedient servant and fast friend

Johannes Kip – this 1st day of April, 1709

Me and My Mourning Ring

HARRIET MCDONALD

The burden of death hangs heavy over all of us. You more than most, I suspect. The funniest thing is that you'll never go away, not really. It doesn't end when you die, it carries forward. All of your quirks, your preferences; like how you take your tea or what books you like to read. You'll elude my every thought, every day for the rest of my life, every act or notion will remind me of you.

Everyone's grieving period was brief. I know you would have liked it that way, for people to focus on the joy your life brought rather than mourn the loss of it. But we genuinely cannot help it, the light has vanished. So has the air. I find myself clutching at my chest desperately as my lungs take in as much air as they can, while I feel something claw its way out of my heart. My love, mostly, because what is grief if not the residual love you feel toward another?

I do not know where to put all of this love for you. It has no other recipient, it has only been created and stored for you. You are also the only one who can destroy it, these unseen bonds of energy that connect us even in death.

I don't fear what comes next, I revel in it, for I know one day we shall meet again under the same circumstances, at the same place, at the same time. I look forward to that day wholeheartedly, I count the days as I lie in anticipation, I am filled with longing, I wait to be enthralled by your call. Your song.

But until then it is only me and my mourning ring. Your portrait is shiny and gorgeous, it is lit from within; like your soul has been passed directly into this piece. My mind remembers what my body cannot. If I focus hard enough, the ring makes me feel like I'm holding your hand for the very last time, all over again. I can hear your raucous laughter down the corridors, the piano's tune coming up the stairs and your smile as I look in the mirror. I miss you. God, I miss you far too much.

I bet you're pitying me right now, pitying my struggle, pitying the barriers I've put up. The more people you let into your life, the chances are they are more likely to leave. You've taught me that.

I caress the ring often, I imagine it as your hair. Your tightly curled hair slipping softly through my fingers like sand. Just as you slipped past my hands now, regardless of all the stalling and grasping of time I can manage.

I may never get over you, I may never be able to live fully again, I may never be the same man I once was. But I can promise I'll never forget you, I'll never not carry my memories of you everywhere, I'll always think of you. This is a promise I swore in marriage and I promise I will keep. Till Death Do Us Part. Always and forever.

Wholly and truly.

But until we reunite once more, under the same circumstances, at the same time and at the very same place, I wave goodbye to you once more. It is time for you to rest.

And as the dirt hits the coffin and tears flood my tired eyes, I realise that for now, it is only me and my mourning ring.

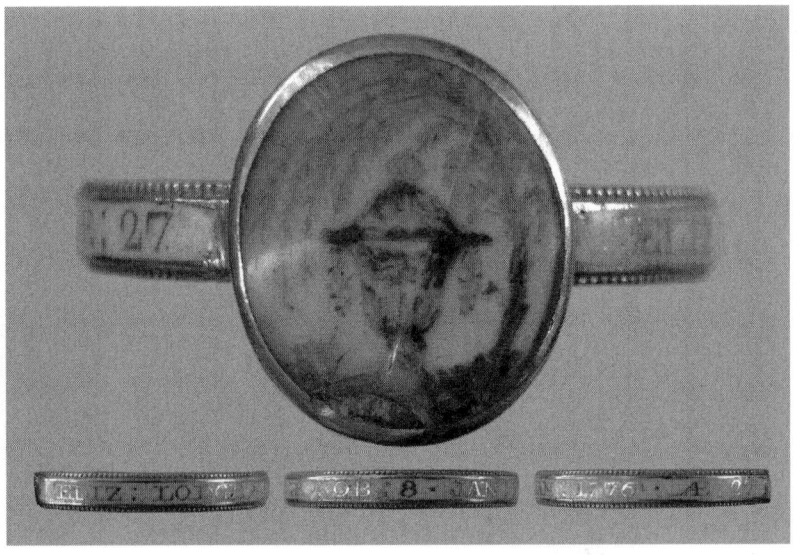

An exquisite gold and enamel mourning ring, inscribed Elizabeth Lodge and dated January 1776. She was 27 when she died. These were made and worn in order to remember someone who had passed away

Eighteenth century

Accession Number G266

ᚦᚢᚱ ᛏᚱᚨᛗᛁᚾ
ᚺᛖᛏᚱᚨ |
ᛚᛟᚢᛖ ᛏᚺᛖ
ᚱᚨᛏᛖᚾ ᚠᛏ
ᛏᚺᛖᛚᛟᚱᛁᛏᛖ
ᚦᛚᚢᛖᛚᚦ

Runes

HENRY DAVIES

My name is
Henry. I
love the
runes at
the Corinium
Museum

Amalie Zuckerkandl*

GRAHAM POWELL

She said, rubbing at the numbers on her arm,
That his death had been a disappointment to her
Although, as far as she could remember,

The way he'd fashioned her shoulders and her neck,
With a choker made of black to frame
The blush-pink of her cheeks and steadfast gaze,

Had, despite the absence of her gown
And lack of arms, left her with a look of
Permanence, of dignity and of calm

Which, had he lived, would have been embellished
With a bank of poppies, summer flowers
To reflect the bloom within her flesh

But, now that he has died, has left her dressed
In nothing but a sackcloth daubed with paint
To show, with ashy scratch marks on the walls,

What might have been within the teeming furnace
Of his brain in those last few days, or hours,
Before his eyes were closed and left her

Incomplete – this portrait of a lady quite
Undone – captured and abandoned in a room
With all that is to come as yet unknown

* Gustav Klimt's portrait of Amelie Zuckerkandl was left unfinished at the time of his death in 1918. Amelie Zuckerkandl was murdered in 1942 at Belzec extermination camp.

Sonnet for The Minoan Honeybees Pendant*

MARGARET ROYALL

Minoan beauty, gold as molten sun,
an ancient gem depicting two small bees,
fine granulations challenging to hone
for craftsmen working in the years BC.
Clasping a honeycomb they seek to place
a drop of honey furtively inside;
their bodies inward-turned, their wings outstretched
perfection focused on minutiae.
Bees at that time were held in sanctity,
creating bold connections between Earth
and underworld, held high in Greek esteem,
though small in size, slim-framed with fragile girth.

This masterpiece is still revered today –
a gem of Cretan history, here to stay.

---

* *Minoan Honeybees* – a famous pendant dating back to the Middle Bronze Age (1800—1600 BC) and today considered the most famous piece of Minoan jewellery. Presently on display at the Heraklion Archaeological Museum, Crete.

For Whom the Death Bell Tolls

AMARIS CHASE

A pitiful scream woke me up, piercing the chilled night air and the steady drum of rain against the brittle window. In my half slumber I tried to work out where it was coming from … It was only when my son, Finn, entered swiftly into my room that I realised that I was the source of that painful wail.

"Are you alright, Father?" He came over and held me gently like a child. Confused, I looked around the shadows of my room, my eyes adjusting to the darkness illuminated by a sliver of the crescent of the moon. Were there hidden dangers lurking in the bleakness of my room? I had an overwhelming sense that someone was waiting to take my life.

I clutched Finn briefly. "It was just that dream again," I assured Finn. I felt his body stiffen slightly. Did he believe in superstition? It was my turn to soothe him as the child that he was, and always would be to me. "It was just a dream, son, I didn't mean to frighten you."

Finn left eventually but I knew that I would not return to sleep. Fear had consumed me. I replayed the dream in my head … it was the third time in as many weeks that it had occurred, but this time the dream had ended differently.

In the dream, it was a sunny day, and I was walking

towards a church with other villagers, but not within my own village. I could see the bell tower, but no matter how much we walked, the church always looked the same distance away. I walked directly behind three women in widow's weeds. Perhaps it was a funeral procession I was part of? The woman in the centre was short and stout, and the women on either side were tall and lean, emphasizing the matriarch in the middle.

Suddenly the three women stopped dead in their tracks and turned to stare at me. The faces of the taller women were hidden behind a veil, but the woman in the centre lifted the filmy fabric. *That face…*

The church bells tolled thrice, and in that time, I was compelled to look at that face. What would have otherwise been a matronly face had the pallor of death, and stared at me with just the whites of the eyes like gleaming opals, no pupils to indicate sight and life. I felt those lifeless eyes bore into my soul with malignant intent.

On the third stroke, the woman dropped her veil and all three turned around. We would continue walking, and again they would stop and turn to stare at me just as the bells tolled three times. This cycle repeated three times in all. After the third time the bells had tolled, I would wake up screaming, and the image of those opal eyes and the haunting sound of the tolling bells wouldn't leave me for the rest of the day. Those bells had not tolled for a normal church service, for they only tolled thrice.

Only this time the dream had continued. After the second round of the bell tolling, my shadowy companions and I actually reached the church. The women were not able to pass the yew tree that marked the southern boundary of the graveyard, the side where funeral processions entered the church. Folklore had it that yew trees were planted in graveyards to stop spirits roaming outside the church, and to stop evil spirits from entering. These three women must be devils in disguise, I thought, if they could not pass the yew tree. Instead they formed a line against the wall of the graveyard and pointed in unison to an overgrown, neglected grave that leant forward with age.

I understood the instruction and walked to the headstone. I walked towards it with tension pounding in my head. I pushed away the weeds to read the inscription, but it was blank, no sign of ever having anything inscribed on it, just a plain stone waiting to be carved. I understood that this grave was for me, waiting for my name, date of demise, and my epitaph. That's when I woke up screaming like a banshee.

What did the dream mean? Was it just a recurring nightmare? Or was it a portend? I was not a religious man, I had sinned, but no more than any other common man of my time. I had never taken another life, nor another man's money. Should I be afraid of death? I had never feared it before, but as I grew older, I became more aware of my mortality and the fear of the unknown as to what lay waiting for me when I died.

The shadow of death followed me for the rest of the day, but the feeling of foreboding slowly left me. The dream did not return, and I soon stopped thinking about it.

Then some weeks later, as Finn and I exchanged news with friends in the tavern, the church bells started pealing unexpectedly and with urgency. Silence descended in the tavern.

"Who can be ringing the bells?" asked someone, as we all knew the only bellringers in the village were sitting with us, and the vicar had ridden out a few miles to read the last rites to an isolated parishioner.

"It must be kids playing a prank," suggested another voice.

"No, only a trained man can ring a bell like that," said one of the bellringers.

"It must be evil spirits taking over our church!"

I think they said it as a joke, but it hung heavy in the air until someone else suggested nervously, "We should stay here until the bells stop ringing …"

Then I knew, those bells rang for me.

"Nonsense! I'll find out who is behind this!" I said with determination, the tavern being stunned into silence at my outburst.

"Father, no!" protested Finn. I shook off his restraining arm and marched out of the tavern, and as soon as I stepped outside the bells stopped ringing. I heard mummering behind me.

When I reached the path leading to the church I stopped abruptly as I saw the three women in widow's weeds, waiting with their backs to me. They began to walk onwards slowly, I followed behind and matched their pace. Anger now replaced fear, I wanted answers, but I felt I was in a trance, mesmerised by their movements.

I barely registered the breathlessness next to me. My boy Finn had run after me. I ignored him as he pleaded, "Father, please come back! Everyone in the tavern is fearful for you!"

The bells tolled once.

The women stopped, I stopped, Finn caught his breath.

The bells tolled a second time.

The women turned to look at me.

The bells tolled a third time.

The middle woman lifted her veil. That mottled skin of the deceased, those opal, lifeless eyes of my dreams. Then she turned away again and the women continued walking. I followed, with Finn next to me.

"What are you looking at Father?"

"Do you not see them? The three devils from my dream?"

"But there is no one there, Father!"

The bells tolled once.

The women stopped, I stopped, Finn stopped.

The bells tolled a second time.

The women turned to look at me.

The bells tolled a third time.

The lifting of the veil, that face of death. Again the three of them turned around and carried on walking.

More pleading from Finn. "They torment me in my dreams and now they taunt me in life," I responded angrily as I continued to follow these demons.

Now we had almost reached the church, the yew tree in sight.

The bells tolled once.

The women stopped, I stopped, Finn stopped.

The bells tolled a second time.

The women turned to look at me.

The bells tolled a third time.

No lifting of the veil this time, just the three pointing in unison towards the graveyard. I understood I should enter the graveyard, but not alive, and with that I felt an icy grip clutch my heart and squeeze hard, Finn's alarmed shouting like a whisper as I left this mortal coil.

THE YOUNG MAN waited for the mourners to leave the freshly dug grave before studying the headstone for a last time.

He had paid for it to be engraved with the following epitaph on advice of the clergy, to ask help from his ancestors to escort his father to the afterlife and prevent any demon from claiming his father's soul:

> *To the spirits of the departed. Guide the spirit of*
> *your descendant to safety. His heir, Finn Cartwright,*
> *has erected this stone*

A Roman Love Story

ROSE LEICESTER

The story of Barates and Regina had been lost since the 2nd century CE and might never have been found but for the fact that in 1878 a labourer, digging a foundation for a factory wall in South Shields, struck a stone with his pick. The stone was elaborately carved and, where it was lifted from the ground, broke into four pieces. When the pieces were taken to the town museum, they fitted together perfectly.

The artefact that had been discovered was a memorial stone to a Roman lady whose face had unfortunately been hacked away, it is not certain when but possibly by the labourer's pick. The sculptor had very skilfully and beautifully carved the drapery of her robe. She is sitting in a wicker chair, holding a distaff and spindle in her lap and, in her right hand, she has a jewellery box. She wears a necklace and bracelets and her hair is in ringlets.

There is a basket containing balls of spun wool at her left side. The distaff and spindle symbolise the feminine virtues of house and home. There is also a halo round her head, showing that she has died and has now become supernatural. The Latin inscription on the tombstone reads:

DM REGINA LIBERTA ET CONIUGE
BARATES PALMYRENUS NATIONE
CATUALLAUNA AN XXX

The translation is *"To the spirits and to Regina, his freed-woman and wife, a Catuvellaunian by tribe, aged 30. Barates of Palmyra set this up."* There is one line in the Palmyrene language, it says "Regina the freedwoman of Barates, alas." The two languages on one stone is unique in Britain. The stone is a metre high and carved in sandstone.

Barates' own tombstone was found not far away from Regina's. In the 2nd Century CE, he was a trader in military flags for the Roman army and came from Palmyra, a very important and wealthy city, now in modern Syria. At the time the tombstone was made he was living in Arbeia, then called Lugudunum, which guarded the main sea route to Hadrian's Wall. Arbeia was a key fort and supply base for the army.

Palmyra was on the Silk Road, a trade route which connected the east and the west. The north of England always was so very different to Palmyra. Barates must have missed the warmth of his homeland, as well as the spices and perfumes, compared to the cold and rain of the northern weather, making it necessary to wear thick woollen clothes.

Barates had found Regina in the south of England as he travelled on his trading route on his way north. The name Regina means Queen and she belonged to the Catuvellaun tribe, which is now the area of Bedfordshire, Buckinghamshire and Herefordshire, and the capital of that tribe was Verulaneum, now St Albans. Barates bought

Regina as a slave and took her to Arbeia. He then later fell in love with her and freed her, married her and made her the lady of his house, so she would now have her own slaves to command.

Judging by the wording on the tombstone, their relationship seemed to have been a happy one and it sounds as if Barates was very sad to have lost Regina. He put on the tombstone in Palmyrene "alas" which makes it more poignant that she died at the age of 30. No one knows how she died, whether it was in childbirth or through illness or accident, as no bones have been found near the stone. Additionally, no one really knows how she felt about being taken away from her family to be sold as a slave and moving north.

The magnificence of the carving shows that Barates was wealthy enough to afford to set up this elaborate stone but one would like to think that this memorial shows his affection and love for Regina and it is hoped that she felt the same about him. It is sad that we cannot see her face but it may well have been as beautiful as the rest of her gravestone.[1] It is hoped that, during their time together, they were happy and in love until she died and that she was always his Queen.

---

[1] Regina's tombstone is in the *Arbeia South Shields Roman Fort and Museum.*

Genii Cucullati

GRAHAM POWELL

Under a cowl of darkness
three of them maybe four
scurrying down pathways

turning corners under arches
disappearing before we're certain
we've seen anything at all

we hear their distant whispers
in the shadows of the moonlight
with the empty sandalled scamper of their
      fast-departing feet

they bid us not to follow
draw fingers to their chapped and bearded lips
pull fast their hoods noose-tight about their necks

and leave us in a swirling shroud of cloth
with their faces looking backwards
to the scraping of a slowly closing door

the rusted bolt is housed
the key is turned and taken from the lock
we watch the dampness slacken from each footprint
      as it fades

hear the shuffling of the rootling midnight beast
the flapping of a bat wing in the dark
the mewling of an infant in its dreams

and rubbing hard our sore and wearied eyes
smell the warmth at last of freshly risen bread
and tell ourselves there's been nothing here at all

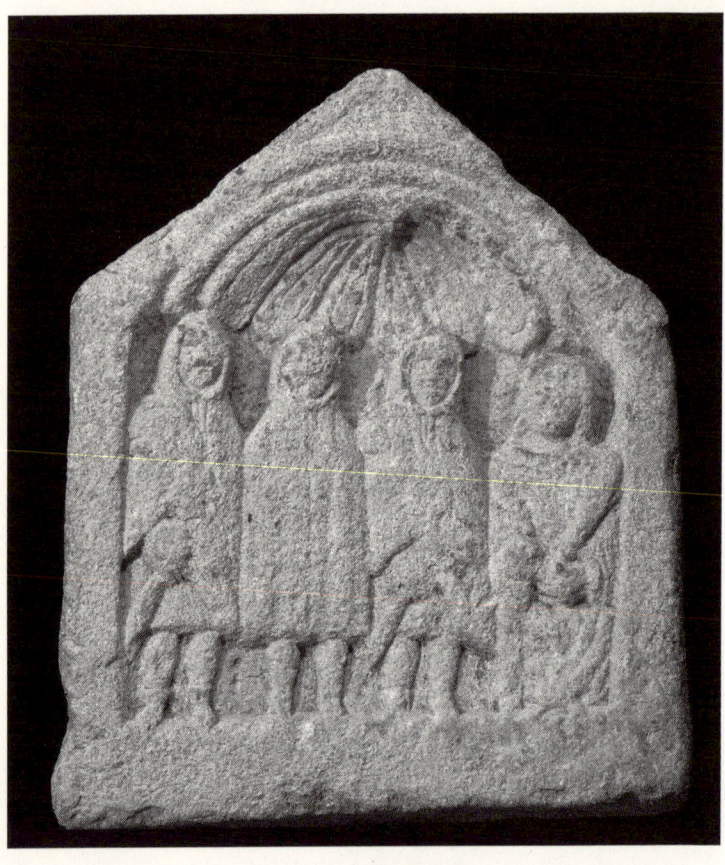

A Roman votive relief depicting three hooded spirits and a seated goddess. Found during the building of the new police station in Cirencester in 1964. The Genii Cucullati were one of the local cults of Corinium, alongside the Mother Goddesses. Little is known about the worship and ritual surrounding these figures, but many reliefs depicting their likenesses have been found in the area

Roman

Accession Number A350

The Gold Coin

LUCY DALGLEISH

I see you, looking at me. Can't help yourself.

I am a gold coin. I've heard some people say I'm not very big, but since when did size equate to power? I can tell you want me, as you lean in to take a closer look through the glass. Even if you don't realise it, you do. I reach into your soul, that very dark part of your soul, where the hoarding greed lives and you want me. My golden reflection in your eyes says it all, my glint, my gleam, as your eyes light up and you want to reach out and take me and keep me for yourself. You want to stash me away in some woven purse, or to hold me in the cusp of your palm, and stroke me, like they used to. Come closer whilst I whisper this. I have heard that there are bigger, more shiny objects in this place. I also know that next to me are other coins. Lesser coins, silver or younger. No names on them. They cannot match me because I am that rare artefact, inscribed by our great tribal father, Bodvoc. I am older than those brooches and pendants, with their blood red garnets, I surpass them all as the original. The OG (I listen to everything you all say). As the best. Stay a while, behold my brilliancy, and let me tell you more.

The King

From the minute I was minted I was special. (I do not have

time to tell you about my formation in the stars, how the meteor collided with earth, eons before man and how my home was for many years a dark and dreary place. I shall save that story for another day. For now, be satisfied that I was brought up from the depths in hands the size of boulders. That man, silent and stern, instantly knew of my remarkable qualities.)

It was at Bagendon that my transformation began. I passed from solid to liquid in temperatures as hot as the sun (I could bear a great deal of heat back then), and in my fluid state I flowed from the crucible becoming a mere flan. I thought that was it, fated to remain a plain gold coin. But out of them all I was chosen and struck with an iron die of exquisite design, by the most talented metalworkers of the age. One side the sacred horse, see the intricate detail of three tails. Three was a magic number even in those days. On my other side, you can't see it from where you are standing, I am irrefutably and irreplaceably branded with our King's name. You may think so what? It is strange to think that little me was (am) so precious, when coins are such a common thing these days. The great Bodvoc was my king and tribal ruler of the Dobunni, who, let me tell you, were the fiercest and most intelligent tribe of all of this island. I may be a little biased. But look at me!

Bodvoc caressed me in my cooled state in his brutish hand, the fingers stained with green and soil. He held me high and I cast a thousand glittering rays across his great broad forehead and illuminated the bristles on his nose. I could see the flecks of amber in his brown eyes that told of battles and victories, of blood spilled. His smokey scent. He laughed and put me between his teeth, breath stinking of rotten venison and bit me. I gave him such intense pleasure.

The Maiden

One sunny day I was pressed into a hand, soft and warm. A young maiden, eyes wide, pink mouth astonished, with flowers around her head, a light green cloth round her shoulders. She smelt of wet earth and willow and clutched me tight to her breast, then opened her hand to gaze upon me once more, then closed me against her bosom again, over and over. I could feel her heart quicken each time.

The maiden held me all that day and night as she danced and sang until she was taken to bed by her man. But still she would not let me go. The next day, she kissed me and took me to the river, singing all the while. There she put me on a rock as she dug down into the riverbed for the soft clay beneath. Deftly she shaped a small pot, let it harden by the fire in her home, and put me in the middle of it on a bed of straw, sealing me inside. Where she put me in her home, I cannot say. I was in the dark. But occasionally she would pick me up and rattle me, singing again. And then I would be still for some time more.

Time passed until one day I realised I had not heard the singing for quite some time. Next thing I knew - smash! The pot lay in pieces around me. The woman was no where to be seen. That man, I knew he couldn't resist me, no one can. I do that, you see, get under your skin. Make you want me. I was in his hot sweaty hand. I could hear his panting. I knew in that instance that I would never again nestle against the warm skin of that maiden, see the constellation of freckles across her cheeks, or feel the vibrations of her heart.

The Priest

Oh, the Priest. I can't forget him. I was given to the priest (you would probably call him a druid), in exchange for a blessing of abundance and renewal for a tanner, so that his animal skins would produce the best leather. There was a look on the priest's face, furtive, craven, as he closed his greasy palm over me. I could hear his amulets rattling like a dead man walking. He did, at least, conduct the ritual. In a sacred grove of hazel and oaks, I was laid on a bed of moss and twigs and bones (goat, I think) at the foot of the tallest tree, on top of a ridge line. It looked over the valley to the river snaking in the distance. With his fungal feet either side of me, he raised his arms to the sky, to the woodland gods and goddesses, muttering, then he turned and swooped away like a raven. Could have been worse. There was no live sacrifice, animal or otherwise.

I watched the sun goddess, as she touched each blade of grass and leaf and shimmering bark with her luminous glow in a moment of perfect harmony. And I have to admit, right then, she was more golden than even I. As she disappeared, the trees become sculptural, dark silhouettes against her last light. Clusters of spiders began spinning their threads of silk. The midges and gnats, like a sparkling dust, danced in the gloaming. The undulations and contours of the landscape were all accentuated by their own shadows, everything was in deep relief, magnified by light and shade. The moon, rose and in the gaps of the canopy I could see from whence I had once come, a twinkling against the blackening sky.

The scoundrel returned that very night. The priest flitted, ghost-like, his white robe concealing his face. I was pinched, squeezed between his fingertips as if he almost dared not touch me, perhaps for fear of the goddesses, or fear he might not be able to give me up. Under the milky light he met with a woman, a witch, who lifted her cape and dress, blessing him with her full abundance. I believe in their act of taking me, they cursed me. For some time, the witch kept me in her armpit, with the lice.

The Farmer

The farmer kept me under his tongue for a little while. Until his daughter stitched him a squirrel skin to hang on leather tie around his neck. This was far more agreeable for both of us. The stitching was not her finest work and a nick of light fissured through the gap. In his house, hay-dusty, the air thick with bleats and that sour grassy smell of wool, I heard the farmer talking, of his plans for more sheep, a bigger holding, a new wife. His hand would absent-mindedly stroke the squirrel skin. I could read his thoughts, yes, he wanted more of me. I was his security, but I tormented him. I could tell. In his sleep he would jerk and grasp the squirrel hide, lashing out at battles past, and only with me in his grip could he slumber peacefully again. He was a kind man, but a greedy one.

The journey to market was long and uncomfortable. I was jostled around and with each step the stitching worked itself looser and looser. I tried to hold myself back, stop myself from getting closer to the abyss of light. But then I was falling. Spinning. Horse, Bodvoc, horse, Bodvoc, landing horse up in a rutted muddy track. I watched as the farmer blundered on with his flock. And I realised, I was lost.

The Pig

I lay, despondent for quite some time. Days passed, nights passed. Light penetrated the woods like spears and I was confident it would not be long before my golden radiance was seen. But alas, I was passed by and no one glanced down. I was scuffed and kicked to the side and lay unseen under the brambles and hazelnuts. I almost don't want to tell you this, but I was set upon by a rapacious beast. The giant roguish porcine guzzled down all in its path with ruthless efficiency. Me included. I cannot tell you how deeply unpleasant it all was and how my stoicism in the face of this adversity was quite extraordinary. I shall spare you the details, the things I witnessed, you've gone a little pale. Suffice to say, I took control of that swine. Commanded the pig to expel me, and it did, deep in the woodland. I lay for a long time in that grove. Buried under twigs and leaves and soil and I thought that was it. With each passing Samhain I fell a little deeper into the ground.

Found

And there I lay in the darkness, back from whence I came. For how long, I shall never know, for what is time to me? It could have been a blink of an eye, or a million years, for I am made from the universe. My form, my atoms and particles have no forwards and no backwards and existed long before man. And most likely will be here after too. I'll confess though, it was a dark and barren time for me. Who knows what turbulent events happened over my head, what troubled and fractured history took place. I did start to feel a little sad for myself. Forces and pressure nibbled away at me, roughened my once smooth edges so that now I am a little dishevelled. No! I don't want your pity. That's all been and gone now.

Wait! Don't move on. Let me hold your attention a little longer, let your eyes examine every little detail of me. Soak me up. Can you feel me watching you, as you watch me? Can you feel that tingle, that prickle under your skin? That's me, coursing through your veins. I'm doing that to you.

It's almost closing now. Tonight when you eventually go home, you'll find your thoughts drift back to me. You won't be able to help yourself. As I said, size is no measure of power.

Come and see me again tomorrow. I'll tell you how I was found.

You'll be back tomorrow. I know you will. I will be waiting for you.

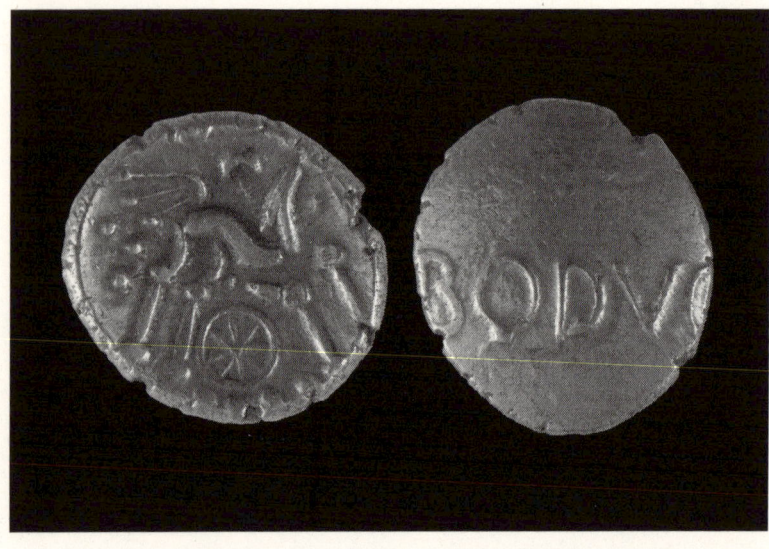

A late Iron Age gold coin, or stater, depicting a triple-tailed horse. The area around Lechlade and Fairford seems to have been used for large scale horse rearing prior to the Roman invasion and this design appears to be the symbol of the local tribe, the Dobunni. The writing on the reverse would have fully spelled BODVOC, the name of the local king, however the die was misaligned so the full text was not transferred

Iron Age

Probably minted at Bagendon

Accession Number 1982/135

ABOUT THE
CORINIUM MUSEUM

Park Street, Cirencester GL7 2BX

Corinium Museum holds large and internationally significant collections of archaeology, social and rural history. It has arguably the finest and most extensive Romano-British collection relating to a town and its hinterland in the world.

Plan your visit: **coriniummuseum.org**

Open daily

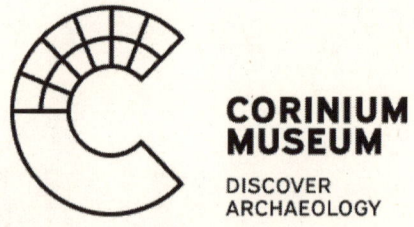

A NOTE FROM THE EDITOR

This book has been produced in collaboration with the Corinium Museum in Cirencester, and in particular my thanks go to Museum Director, Emma Stuart. It has been no small feat for us to bring together such a fabulous range of talented writers and photographs of the artefacts, while also fulfilling our respective roles on the subcommittee for the first Cirencester History Festival in 2024. This book has been published to tie in with that festival.

I am naturally enthusiastic about history. My background is archaeological illustration, formerly working with one of the foremost national units in the UK. I was present in 2011 when the Roman cockerel figurine was brought in by the field archaeologist who had discovered it. I remember the murmur which went around the office saying that one of the team at the Bridges Garage site in Cirencester had uncovered something special and they were bringing it in.

They were right. The mud-encrusted artefact cradled in their hands truly was special.

I was also the lucky person who was tasked with producing the technical drawings of the cockerel – recording it for archival purposes – after it had returned from the conservator. It was such a challenging form with curves and intricate enamelling that it took three long days to draw. I became one of only a handful of people who have handled the object (with great care!) since it was deposited almost 2000 years ago in a child's grave by people who must have loved the young person very much.

It is at times like these when the span of millennia fall away, and I realise the people of the past were just like us.

In the present, I was certain that the idea of inviting writers and poets to respond to the objects creatively would lead to new and exciting ways of engaging with the past. As I edited this collection, I stepped into a world of short stories, memoir shorts, and poems which each relate to a historical object in very different ways.

Sometimes beautiful, sometimes sinister, and frequently touched with a powerful sense of loss – each of the authors has found a means of bringing the voices of the past to life, or giving voice to the objects themselves. Vivid, relatable, and thoroughly mesmerising.

Lorna Brookes
Crumps Barn Studio

Soldiers and spies, children and animals. A town with an army at its gates

An informative and accessible history of the English Civil War battle, told in short stories by young writers, from the perspective of the people who witnessed it

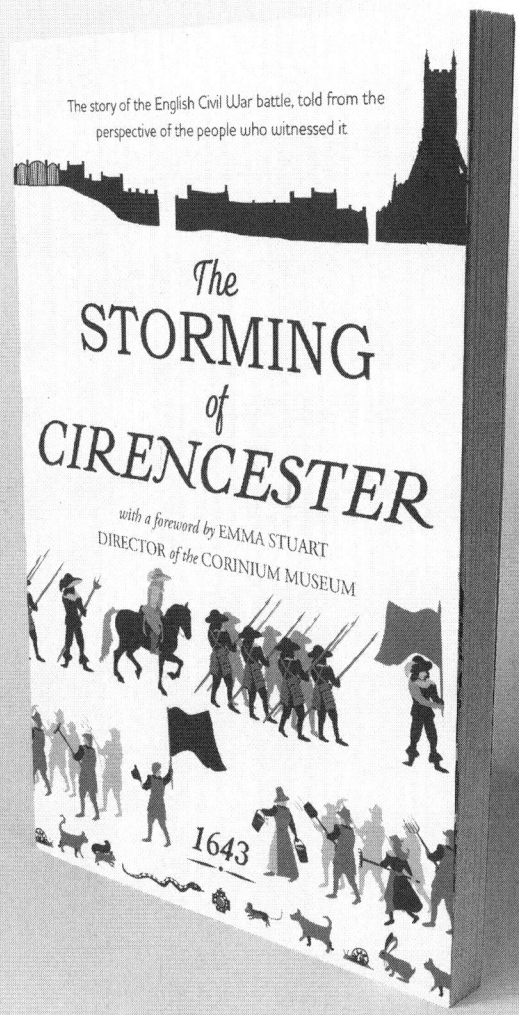

in collaboration with the CORINIUM MUSEUM

If you loved this book, you'll love
our other anthologies ...

Spooky Ambiguous

Ghosts and vampires, zombies and werewolves. Full of the spooky and the gothic, fairy tales and poetry, this is a brilliant and intriguing collection where nothing and no one is as they seem

ISBN 9781915067128

The Wild Night Sky

Stars and planets, vast skies and new horizons. Full of mystery and adventure, true memories and poetry, this is a brilliant and far-ranging collection about our present and future relationship with space

ISBN 9781915067258

Home Ground

Trolls and pookas, wild woodlands and fairy meadows. Full of the mysterious and the gothic, myths and memoir, this is a captivating and intriguing collection inspired by the magic within a landscape the authors know well

ISBN 9781915067487

The Storming of Cirencester

Soldiers and spies, children and animals. The 1643 battle for Cirencester during the English Civil War is captivatingly retold from the perspective of the people who witnessed it

ISBN 9781915067661

Crumps Barn Studio
www.crumpsbarn.online